# Beading
## 200 Q&A

# Beading
## 200 Q&A

Questions answered on everything from basic stringing
to finishing touches

Dorothy Wood and Ashley Wood

**For Sorrel, who is always right.**

A Quantum Book

Copyright © 2010 Quantum Publishing

First edition for North America and the Philippines published in 2010 by
Barron's Educational Series, Inc.

All inquiries should be addressed to:
Barron's Educational Series, Inc.
250 Wireless Boulevard
Hauppauge, New York 11788
**www.barronseduc.com**

ISBN-13: 978-0-7641-6359-3
ISBN-10: 0-7641-6359-0

Library of Congress Control Number:  2010921562

This book is published and produced by
Quantum Books
6 Blundell Street
London N7 9BH

QUMBEQA

Project Editor: Samantha Warrington
Production: Rohana Yusof
Photographer: Marcos Bevilacqua
Design: Andrew Easton
Publisher: Sarah Bloxham

All images are the copyright of Quantum Publishing,
apart from p.77 which is copyright of Quarto Publishing.

Printed in China by Midas Printing International Ltd.

9 8 7 6 5 4 3 2 1

# CONTENTS

*Introduction*                                                    *6*

Chapter 1:    Beads                                    8

Chapter 2:    Findings                                30

Chapter 3:    Threads and Wires                       54

Chapter 4:    Tools and Equipment                     72

Chapter 5:    Stringing and Knotting                  90

Chapter 6:    Bead Weaving                           106

Chapter 7:    Bead Looming                           150

Chapter 8:    Wirework                               174

Chapter 9:    Other Ways to Use Beads                204


*Useful Information*                                             *221*

*Index*                                                         *224*

# INTRODUCTION

Beading has a history stretching back thousands of years; no other art form has quite this long a history, other than cave painting. This is because beads tend to be made of materials that are lasting; they don't rot away like fabrics and papers. Early man was not able to use metal or ceramics, but used bone and horn beads; those made of shells or coral have survived well.

The first beads were shells and stones with a naturally formed hole, and were strung on vines. Later beads used pieces of hollow bone, and then as stone tools developed, beads could be carved and pierced, allowing them to be made from teeth, shells, seeds, and horns.

Beads carved from animal bones, teeth, and horns were totems, believed to hold the power of the animal they had belonged to. A hunter might wear the tooth of a tiger or bear to give him added skills and bravery, or use hollow bone beads from a deer or horse to draw their spirit to him on the hunt.

Native tribes used different materials to make beads – some drilled holes in seeds, plant pods, and nuts, while others made beads from clay and painted them with crude paints. Later beads were worked with metal tools, or even made from polished metal. Beads were still strung and used as totems for protection, but were also stitched to fabric or used in sacred rites.

Three thousand years ago glass was discovered, and beads made of glass became very popular and spread across the continents of Africa and Asia. The Egyptians discovered how to color glass beads and made beautiful and intricate designs. They used different colored glass to signify different gods, status, and states of mind; Egyptians believed that beads of particular types and colors put together in a particular way could ensure health and happiness or a place in the next world.

The Romans believed pearls would make the goddess Isis watch over them, and used beads to create the first calculator: the abacus. They traded beads across the empire, even bringing beads from as far away as Indonesia. Semi-precious stones were much loved by the Romans, and they developed many techniques for machining and polishing them. Glass beads were produced all over the Roman Empire and many colors and designs could be found; it was during this period that the process of glassblowing was developed, creating even more exciting beads.

Even the marauding Vikings made beautiful beads; they created amazing colors in their glass beads as well as beautiful designs. The beads themselves were not as elaborate as those made at the same time by other peoples, but they were arranged in really beautiful designs. Viking amulets, necklaces, and bracelets survive to the present day.

In the late 1800s, wily clothing makers realized that beading clothing, shoes, and accessories meant that it was possible to charge huge sums for clothing. Aristocrats were willing to wait for months for intricate stitched designs on everything from dresses to dance slippers. Royalty had magnificent and beautiful clothing decorated with precious stones and metals, which emphasized their power and wealth.

In the early twentieth century, the Edwardians and Victorians continued to wear bead-encrusted fabrics and elaborate jewelry. Even the "Flappers" of the 1920s wore layers of long, beaded necklaces with their boyish haircuts and clothing. The Flappers were also the first to experiment with plastic beads — made of Bakelite — but it was not until after the wars that costume jewelry became really popular.

With the plastic revolution, costume jewelry became popular and plastic beads widespread. Beaded fabric became less and less popular, and the cheaply produced plastic beads could be used to mimic more expensive semiprecious beads such as turquoise.

Today, beads are traded around the world and it is possible to find African, Indian, Native American, and Venetian beads among many others in every day fashion. Beading is enjoying a renaissance, and the old techniques and styles are being updated and improved, with the fantastic new materials available to the modern beader.

In addition to easy access to a wide range of beads, both online and in your local bead shop, you have greater access to beading and jewelry than any other group in history. For the first time, beading has hit the catwalk in a big way, and has been filtering into mainstream fashion; now there are beautiful examples of beading in almost every clothing shop.

This book will answer your questions on the techniques and materials available, so that you can take the inspirations from the shops and make your own fabulous pieces. Keep an eye on the latest jewelry fashions to find amazing color combinations and new ways of combining beads. We hope you find this book helpful, and hope that it inspires you to continue learning and creating with beads.

1   What is a bead?

2   How are large beads sold?

3   What shapes of beads are available?

4   What is the difference between glass and lampwork beads?

5   What is the best crystal bead?

6   How do I identify real pearls?

7   What other natural beads come from the sea?

8   What are the benefits of beads made from wood and seeds?

9   Are bone and horn beads legal?

10  What is a semiprecious stone?

11  What is the difference between polymer clay beads and ceramic beads?

12  How do I choose metal beads?

13  Can I reuse vintage beads?

14  How are seed beads packaged?

15  How do charlottes differ from ordinary seed beads?

16  What is the difference between bugle and hex beads?

17  Why are cylinder beads so special?

18  What other shapes of seed beads are available?

19  How do I choose colors that go together?

20  What is the difference between transparent, opaque, and translucent finishes?

21  What other finishes are available?

# 1

# BEADS

Beautiful beads can be found in different styles and materials all over the world. This chapter gives you an introduction into the types and materials you may encounter.

# Question 1:
# What is a bead?

It sounds rather obvious, but essentially a bead is a decorative object with a hole for stringing. Modern beads are used mainly for decoration and are mostly made of glass. However, looking back through history, beads have been used in many different ways and were formed from all kinds of materials.

Early man used pieces of hollow animal bone on vines as protective charms. When tools for boring holes were created, shells, seeds, stones, and other materials became available to early beaders. Beads were then sewn onto garments, strung into complex jewelry, and used as currency for trade between tribes and nations.

Nowadays, a multitude of different beads are created using techniques that have been discovered and refined through the centuries. You can find out more about the development of beads from various excellent specialized books on the subject as you get more involved in beads and beading. It is also well worth visiting museum exhibitions to get more ideas for jewelry and for making your own beads.

In addition to using manufactured beads from all over the world in your jewelry, think about taking a leaf from ancient man's book; look around you and discover your own beads. Remember, anything with a hole can be classified as a bead, so think about using metal washers, ring pulls, pasta, and sections of plastic drinking straws or buttons!

*BELOW* Beads in a sorting tray.

# Question 2:
# How are large beads sold?

Large beads are defined as those that are not seed beads – i.e., non-glass beads or glass beads larger than 5 mm in diameter. They are usually displayed in large trays in bead shops and are sold individually. The choice can be overwhelming!

Semiprecious stone beads have traditionally been sold in strings, and this method is becoming more popular with other beads, particularly those that are mass-produced and more or less identical. Strings of beads often work out cheaper than buying beads individually, but make sure you check the individual beads to ensure that there are no damaged beads in the center of the string.

Always buy the best quality beads you can afford; large, cheap bags may seem like a bargain, but you may be left with a lot of broken beads. Check the hole before you buy – although it is possible to bore out beads with a blocked hole, it is much quicker and easier to just buy beads with a decent hole in them in the first place. Check the placement of the hole as well; some beads are drilled off-center.

You can buy beads over the Internet in a multitude of styles and sizes from around the world. Often even with postage added, this can work out relatively cheaply. Check the size carefully – beads are measured across the widest point of their diameter – and exactly how many beads you will receive for your money.

Your local bead shop will be able to offer advice and order special items and will allow you to see true colors; often a combination of buying beads online and from your local shop will give you the best result.

*LEFT* Assorted glass beads with varying patterns and colors.

# Question 3:
# What shapes of beads are available?

Although most people think of beads as being small and round, there is a wide array of fantastic shapes available. This list is a description of the more common bead shapes:

- Bicone beads look like two cones stuck together at the base. They can be long and slim or almost disc-shaped.
- Round beads are actually spherical and have a very classical feel.
- Barrel beads are the shape of old-fashioned wooden barrels, with the hole running between the flat ends.
- Disc beads are flat circles with the hole running edge to edge. They allow you to use larger beads without adding too much bulk to your piece.
- Cubes and squares give a more geometric, modern feel to your piece. They also fit together nicely for bead weaving and looming.
- Teardrop-shaped beads are drilled in various ways: drop beads have the hole running lengthwise,

pendants have the hole in the pointed tip, and dagger beads have the hole in the widest part of the bead.
- Cylinder beads can be very long or almost disc-shaped and are drilled lengthwise.
- Doughnut-shaped beads are large, flat circles with a large hole in the center.
- Nugget shapes are a "natural" form; precious stones can often be bought as polished nuggets.
- Oval beads are a smooth, elliptical shape with no edges, and are drilled lengthwise.
- Rhombus beads are cubes drilled from corner to corner and are very eye-catching.
- Tablet beads are rectangular, shaped like flattened bricks.
- Pillow beads have an eye-shaped cross section; they are rectangular, and only have two lengthways edges.

# Question 4:
# What is the difference between glass and lampwork beads?

The most common and easy-to-find beads are made of glass, as it is the most versatile of the materials that beads are made of. Lampwork beads are a specific type of bead made of glass. They are handmade on a workbench using rods or canes of colored glass and a blowtorch. The beads are formed on a revolving metal rod, and it is this winding process that creates the distinctive swirls of color in the bead. Once formed, the bead can be worked with various tools, or crumbled glass added to add texture.

Glass beads are fragile when first made and crack or break easily. To prevent this, they need to be heated and cooled in a kiln; this is called annealing and adds strength to the bead. Cheap glass or lampwork beads made in lots of hundreds are rarely annealed. Buying a big bag of beads cheaply is, therefore, likely to result in a large number of broken beads. Always check that the beads you are interested in are annealed before you buy. Some lampwork beads are now created around metal cores, which does not wear as much as glass when strung on chain; these are called Pandora beads.

*BELOW* A selection of lampwork beads, which are often handmade.

# Question 5:
# What is the best crystal bead?

Crystal beads are not actually made from polished crystals; they are usually made from glass, cut and polished to resemble the natural facets of crystal. "Crystal" is a term used to describe faceted beads – from the most expensive cut glass right down to molded plastic beads.

The most expensive crystals come from the Swarovski Company in Austria; these are the most famous crystals and can be found in most bead shops. A less expensive option is to use crystals from other countries, such as the Czech Republic, or to use fire-polished beads, which are heated at high temperature to create a glossy surface.

The cheapest crystal beads are molded plastic – you can get large tubes of plastic crystals in a range of colors and shapes, and with a variety of different finishes. These crystals are perfect for projects with a large number of beads, such as fringing where high shine is more desirable.

The crystals with the most sparkle are those with the sharpest, most plentiful facets. Sharp facets can cut through stringing material, so you must choose carefully! (See also page 94). A wide range of colors and shapes are available; some of these are more difficult to cut and, therefore, are more expensive. Adding facets and shaping the crystal increases the waste – and the price rises at the same time!

# Question 6:
# How do I identify real pearls?

Pearls come in three basic types; cultured, natural, and fake. Pearls were originally collected in the wild; they are formed when an irritant, such as a parasite, gets into an oyster shell. The oyster coats it in nacre (mother-of-pearl), and gradually, over the years, it turns into a pearl. Originally, pearls were collected by cutting open the oysters, which killed them, and was no guarantee of getting a pearl in the shell. These pearls, called "natural" or "wild" pearls, are rare and very old.

Cultured pearls are formed by placing a shell bead inside the oyster and waiting for at least six months before removing it (without killing the oyster). Because the coating is formed evenly around the shape of the shell bead, it is possible to create pearls of different shapes and sizes. Cultured pearls are either "freshwater" or "saltwater," depending on the type of oyster they are created by. Freshwater pearls tend to be small and bumpy, whereas saltwater pearls are more regularly shaped. High-quality fake pearls have the same luster as real pearls, but come in different shapes and lovely colors.

Reputable sellers will tell you if their pearls are fake; but, if in doubt, rub one against your teeth – real pearls will grate slightly.

## Question 7:
# What other natural beads come from the sea?

The earliest known beads were made from a pair of Nassarius sea snail shells, thought to be 100,000 years old. Shells are still very popular and can be bought in various forms. Complete shells in many sizes can be found; from tiny snail-shell-type shells to large cowry shells, they are drilled and can then be strung like any other bead.

Shell chips are another fantastic natural product – they are usually slightly domed and the edges are ground smooth; they can either be naturally colored or dyed in bright colors. Mother-of-pearl shell chips have the natural outside of the shell on one side and the nacre on the other, and are very striking, particularly when both sides are made part of the design.

Less common, but extremely eye-catching, are slices taken from spiral shells. These can be threaded through the shell spirals or through drilled holes, and make the most of the shell's natural beauty.

Coral beads, made from the cut and polished branches of certain red sea corals are also very beautiful. They range in color from pale pink to deep red, and have been used since ancient Egyptian times. However, the coral takes years to grow, and thought must be given to the damage done to the environment – coral beads should be recycled in new pieces to preserve stocks.

# Question 8:
# What are the benefits of beads made from wood and seeds?

Wooden beads have warmth to the touch unmatched by any other bead. The beads are also light for their size, which allows you to use large statement beads in a piece of jewelry without it becoming unwieldy.

Wooden beads fall into two categories – painted and unpainted. Painted beads are often brightly colored and are particularly associated with children's jewelry. They are very attractive and easily threaded, but it is important to check the quality; cheap beads are often poorly sanded before they are painted and varnished, giving a poor finish, or they may have partially blocked holes.

Unpainted beads are highly polished and varnished to make best use of the wood grain. They may be carved or stained and come in various classic shapes. Certain woods have particular properties to look out for: palm-wood beads have fantastic dark speckles and are a rich amber color; sandalwood has a particularly attractive smell; ebony is very dense and has a beautiful black color. The latter two woods are now a protected resource but can be found in vintage jewelry.

There are a staggering number of seeds and nuts that can be polished and drilled to create beautiful beads. There are particularly strong traditions of creating beads in this way in Africa and India – it is worth checking for naturally sourced beads from around the world, as they are very beautiful and enjoyable to use.

*RIGHT* These wooden beads make use of the natural grain patterns and colors.

# Question 9:
# Are bone and horn beads legal?

Bone beads are legal — as long as they are not from a protected species. They are very attractive and are often carved into shape, surface colored, and then carved again to show the original color.

Horn from cattle or water buffalo is not only legal but also beautiful. Horn can be shaped, carved, stained, and polished and is sometimes used to emulate other materials such as amber. Rhino Horn is illegal, and you should be careful when importing beads to check their origin; if you are found to have imported an illegal animal product, even in error, you may be liable for a large fine.

Ivory is a rather more complex issue — it is illegal to buy unworked ivory of any age, but it is possible to buy antique ivory (pre-1947) if it is carved. It is also possible to buy ivory from animals not on the endangered list, for example, from boars. However, this can be risky, as it is occasionally mislabeled. Be aware that you must have all the correct forms to import any kind of ivory, even antique beads, and the laws on ivory change frequently.

Real tortoise shell is also illegal, but like ivory old pieces from the 1970s can be reused in your own pieces (see also Question 13 for more information on using vintage beads).

*BELOW* Bone and horn beads are usually carved and dyed for added texture.

# Question 10:
# What is a semiprecious stone?

Semiprecious stones or "gemstones" are usually cut-and-polished pure minerals, but some organic materials like amber and jet are also classed as gemstones. Transparent minerals are often cut with facets to add sparkle, whereas opaque stones are often cut into cabochons.

Some semiprecious stones are dyed to produce a more varied range of colors – jade and beryl can be treated in this way to create beautifully colored beads. Gemstones can also be treated in other ways to enhance color and shine. Heat may increase color and clarity, so most aquamarine is treated to give a richer color; blue topaz is almost always irradiated white topaz, while green quartz has also usually been treated in the same way.

*BELOW* An assortment of gemstones of different sizes and shapes.

Semiprecious stones are thought to have healing properties. These can be included in jewelry as beads or polished mineral chips to give a personal twist. Alternatively, birthstones (listed below) are either precious or semiprecious stones, and can be readily included in a special birthday gift.

- January – Garnet (red)
- February – Amethyst (lilac)
- March – Aquamarine (blue-green)
- April – Diamond (white)
- May – Emerald (green)
- June – Pearl (cream)
- July – Ruby (red)
- August – Peridot (pale green)
- September – Sapphire (blue)
- October – Opal (iridescent)
- November – Topaz (yellow)
- December – Turquoise (turquoise)

# Question 11:
# What is the difference between polymer clay beads and ceramic beads?

Ceramic beads are made from a ceramic clay found naturally in the ground, which must be hardened in a kiln at temperatures of at least 1,800 degrees Fahrenheit (1,000 degrees Celsius). Ceramics are coated with special glazes once hardened, and re-fired in the kiln.

Polymer clay is not a mineral at all; it is a plastic based on PVC and can be hardened in a home oven. Further layers can be added once the clay has been hardened, and the surface can be sanded, buffed, or finished with water-based varnish.

Ceramic beads are heavier than polymer clay beads and are cold to the touch. To make ceramic beads you will need a kiln and specialist clay and glaze; a ceramic piece of jewelry, therefore, lacks the personal touch of handmade beads. To make up for this, ceramic beads are available in a multitude of colors and styles from around the world. Polymer clay lends itself to millefiori (a thousand flowers) designs; these were originally created with glass but are very effective with polymer clays. In this technique, polymer clay is rolled into canes arranged into patterns and rolled together into long tubes. Slices are taken from the tube to make flat beads or laid over a base bead to form an intricate floral pattern.

*BELOW* The two central beads are made of polymer clay; the others are glazed ceramic.

# Question 12:
# How do I choose metal beads?

Some people are allergic to the nickel in silver or to the base metals, so you need to consider this when choosing beads. You also need to ensure that your findings match your beads, otherwise the result will look cheap.

Precious metal beads are available in sterling silver or as plated beads in silver or gold. Balinese silver is particularly fine – the crafts people on the island are renowned for their beautiful, high-quality beads.

Base metal beads, such as copper, brass, aluminium, and tin can also be found. Metal beads are created from a variety of techniques: moulding, modeling, and shaping from sheet metal. It is worth looking around at all the possibilities.

Aluminium beads are made as part of the recycling process in India. Aluminium is a relatively light metal that does not corrode or discolor readily, and is an attractive alternative to silver. Brass beads are made all over the world and range from large, pressed metal or molded, hollow beads to small, solid tubes like seed beads.

Another, cheaper alternative to precious metal beads are metalized plastic beads. These are plastic beads with a durable coating, which have the advantages of being both light and inexpensive.

# Question 13:
# Can I reuse vintage beads?

It is hard to define the word "vintage"; in fact, most jewelry sellers will have their own interpretation of the word, so it is best to ask. Generally speaking, "retro" refers to modern items made in an older style; "antique" refers to anything older than about 100 years (although some sellers will class only items made before 1900 or even 1840 as antiques); and "vintage" refers to something made at least 20 years ago. If something is described as "vintage 1940s," it is being described as having been made in the 40s. If it is "vintage 1940s style," it is more likely to be a modern reproduction.

Once you have worked out how old your piece is, you can look at what it is made of. Plastic beads feel warm to the touch, will be relatively light, and don't "clink" when knocked together. Glass, gemstones, and pearls will all clink and feel cold to the touch. If you're still not sure, just decide if you like them – even if you haven't found a bargain string of real pearls or cheap emeralds, if you love the look of the beads you won't be disappointed. Check each bead for damage and check the findings – a very damaged or ugly piece may have an unusual and delightful clasp that can be reused in a more tasteful way.

*BELOW* These old necklaces can be taken apart to provide unusual beads for new jewelry.

# Question 14:
# How are seed beads packaged?

Seed beads are given a size number that roughly equates to the number of beads that fit side by side when lying flat like doughnuts in 1 in. (2.5 cm). They are then packaged in several ways, the most widespread being 3-in. (7.5 cm) tubes, but strings of beads are now becoming more and more popular – seed bead strings are 20 in. (51 cm) long and are sold in hanks of twelve.

Companies package their beads in entirely different ways, so check when buying specific quantities and sizes, as there will also be differences in size and weight between Japanese and Czech beads. In the U.S, Czech beads are often sold on hanks, while Japanese beads are often sold in tubes. The table below gives a rough guide to the number of beads you are likely to get in both 3-in. (7.5 cm) tubes and strung hanks for seed beads of various sizes. As a general rule, the more beads in the tube, the smaller the bead.

| Bead Width (mm) | Bead Size | Beads on 7.9-in. string | Beads in hank | Hank weight | Beads in 3-in. tube | Tube Weight |
|---|---|---|---|---|---|---|
| 3.3 | 6 | 200 | 2400 | 5.9 oz | 150 | 0.46 oz |
| 2.5 | 8 | 260 | 3120 | 3.5 oz | 600 | 0.53 oz |
| 2.2 | 9 | 300 | 3600 | | | |
| 2.0 | 10 | 320 | 3840 | | | |
| 1.8 | 11 | 340 | 4080 | 1.5 oz | 1650 | 0.53 oz |
| 1.3 | 15 | 480 | 5760 | 0.8 oz | 3800 | 0.46 oz |

*RIGHT* The multicolored beads are ordinary seed beads; the silver Charlotte beads catch the light more because of their facet cut.

# Question 15:
# How do charlottes differ from ordinary seed beads?

All seed beads are made using canes of fine-quality glass that is heated until it is red hot and softened, then put into a steel die stamp, which forms the shape of the bead. The hole is then formed with a reciprocating needle. Seed beads are manufactured to a high quality in two main centers worldwide: the Czech Republic and Japan. Japanese beads are known for being uniformly shaped and manufactured; Czech beads are more inconsistent but are of very nice quality.

Charlotte beads have traditionally only been made in the Czech Republic; they are very rare in comparison to ordinary seed beads and are particularly beautiful. After they are produced, a number of the beads are reprocessed and cut so that they have one flat facet. This means the beads sparkle completely differently from normal seed beads.

It is also possible to find two-facet beads which sparkle slightly less. Technically, charlotte beads are only single-facet seed beads of size 1.5 mm diameter (20 beads per inch), although single facet beads are available in various sizes. Recently, Japanese cylinder beads have become available with the single-facet cut, so charlotte cut beads are likely to become much more readily available.

# Question 16:
# What is the difference between bugle and hex beads?

Hex cut beads are standard seed beads with six cut facets on the sides, but they are the same size and diameter as ordinary seed beads. Bugle beads look superficially like large hex beads, but in reality, they are completely different.

Bugles are long, cylindrical tubes that come in different sizes from standard seed beads, and also, confusingly, Japanese bugles come in different sizes to Czech bugles! If you are planning to use bugles alongside seed beads, size 1 bugle = size 12 seed. All other bugles are roughly the same diameter as a size 11 bead. The table below shows the sizes for Japanese and Czech bugle bead lengths.

The other difference between bugles and hexes is that hex beads, along with all other seed beads, are "tumbled" as part of the manufacturing process, which removes sharp edges. Bugle beads, especially those of low quality, retain sharp edges that can cut thread. It is usually better to buy more expensive beads and have fewer discards.

| Bead Size | Czech Bugle Length | | Japanese Bugle Length | |
|---|---|---|---|---|
| | mm | inches | mm | inches |
| 1 | 2 | 3/32 | 3 | 1/10 |
| 2 | 4 | 3/16 | 6 | 1/4 |
| 3 | 7 | 1/4 | 9 | 3/8 |
| 4 | 9 | 3/8 | | |
| 5 | 11 | 7/16 | | |

# Question 17:
# Why are cylinder beads so special?

Cylinder beads are not bugle beads; they are a special type of seed bead made in Japan. They are precision milled to be completely uniform in size and have straight sides, so they lie next to one another smoothly.

Unlike hex beads, cylinder beads are smooth-sided, without facets. They have smooth ends that butt up closely to one another and do not damage thread. Each bead has a larger hole than standard seed beads so that thread can be passed through them several times – perfect for bead looming and weaving – and correspondingly thinner sides, which allows them to sit neatly side by side and form even fabric.

Cylinder beads are often referred to by their trade names in order to distinguish them further from bugle and hex beads. They can be labeled as Delicas, Magnificas, or Antiques.

Look out for Aiko beads, which are considered to be of a higher quality, with only one bead in every 100,000 being discarded during manufacture. Because of this, they are more expensive and harder to get ahold of – only 3kg per day are produced in comparison to more than 500kg of other seed beads. Treasures (from Toho) are another popular cylinder bead.

*BELOW* Cylinder beads of various sizes.

# Question 18:
# What other shapes of seed beads are available?

In addition to rounds, hexes, and bugles, other interesting shapes, finishes, and colors are available. These can be added to your work to create extra texture.

- Drop beads (Magatamas) have an off-center hole, which gives them a bulging teardrop shape. They are sometimes called fringe beads because they are particularly useful as turn beads for fringing. See blue/ green beads in the image below.
- Cube beads are particularly useful for designs that require strength and stability. They also make eye-catching spacer beads and beautiful fringing when combined with round beads. The most common size is 4 mm in diameter with round holes – but you can also find square-holed beads and other sizes. See white beads in the image on the right.
- Triangular beads create a stunning reptile-scale effect when used for herringbone and peyote stitches. Beads are available in sizes 5, 8 and 10 mm in a very wide range of colors and finishes. There are two main types; geometric sharp-sided Toho triangles and more rounded Miyuki triangles. See purple/blue triangular beads in the image.

- Farfalle (Papillon) are a rare Czech seed bead, named after the Italian for "butterfly" because they have two wing shapes on either side of the hole. See rounded white beads in the image below. The beads slot together nicely to create irregular fringing or can be interspersed with round beads to give texture (see also Question 155).

*BELOW* Assortment of beads of various shapes.

# Question 19:
# How do I choose colors that go together?

The key to picking colors that match is the use of a color wheel. The three base colors are red, yellow, and blue; they are called primary colors because they are pure colors. The secondary colors are made from two of the primary colors mixed together – red and yellow making orange; yellow and blue making green; and blue and red making purple. In addition, in beading, black and white are counted as colors – they can be added to enhance the brightness of the colors.

When you are looking for colors, using the wheel allows you to experiment with different mixes.

- Monochromatic schemes use only one color but use paler and darker tones. This mix always looks balanced.

- Analogous schemes use colors next to one another on the color wheel, usually the "cold colors" or "warm colors."

- Complementary colors are opposites on the color wheel: green and red and orange and blue. These mixes are really vibrant.

- Triadic color schemes use three colors that are not next to one another – the primary colors, or the secondary colors. This can look gaudy, but is a very attractive mix if you get your tones right.

- Tetradic color schemes use two pairs of complementary colors. It can be difficult to balance the colors, so you may want to make one the dominant color and tone down the others.

## EXPERT TIP

❝ Use a piece of patterned fabric in unusual colors to help you find beads that contrast nicely — all the hard work of color matching has then been done for you! ❞

# Question 20:
# What is the difference between transparent, opaque, and translucent finishes?

Seed beads, in particular, come in a vast range of finishes, and it can be difficult to work out which is which. To make life even more complex, the finishes can be combined, and there are abbreviations for each finish under which the beads are sold. When you are ordering on the Internet, it is particularly important to know your "Dps" from your "Ops." Transparent beads (Tr) are made of see-through glass and allow light to pass through. They can be found with different color saturations ranging from light (L) to deep (Dp).

- Color saturation means that if you line up transparent beads of the same color next to one another there will be a perceptible difference in the hue. The sequence is light (L); medium (M); dark (Dk) then deep (Dp).
- Opaque beads (Op) are a solid color and don't let light through. The finish is flat and not overly shiny. Opaque beads can also have a rainbow finish (O/R) and give a very good contrast next to shiny or matte beads.
- Translucent beads fall somewhere between the two, and are also described as greasy, opal, or satin beads.

# Question 21:
# What other finishes are available?

Lined beads have a finish applied inside the hole of the bead.
- Black-lined (BL) – adds depth to the bead color.
- Color-lined (Color/L) – has a color inside, often teamed with clear glass for a fresh look.
- Brass-lined (BrL), copper-lined (CL), and silver-lined (SL), or rocaille beads have a metallic lining that makes the bead much shinier. They are often made with a square

hole (SqH) to enhance the shine. Surface finishes are applied to the outside of the bead – they are often applied to rocaille beads for a really luxurious effect.

- Alabaster (AL) – a dense translucent white finish.
- Aurora Borealis (AB) – also known as rainbow, iris, iridescent, and fancy. These beads have highlights in several tones or colors caused by heating in the presence of metal salts.
- Ceylon (Cy) – pearly beads with a colored lining.
- Gloss – high shine finish.
- Luster opaque beads coated with a pearly finish – gold and silver luster beads are particularly beautiful.
- Matte (M) – beads that have been

tumbled to remove the shine from the surface, or treated with an etching compound. Matte Rainbow (M/R) are rainbow beads given a matte coating – the rainbow effect should still be visible. Frosted beads are matte-coated, metal-lined beads. Ghost beads are matte-rainbow, metal-lined beads (this is where abbreviations come in handy).

- Metallic rainbow (Met/R) – appear to be made of metallic colors and are always purple/blue/green/bronze but with differing amounts of each color.

*BELOW* A variety of finishings are available.

## EXPERT TIP

**66 Some finishes wear off over time. This can be prevented in larger beads by coating them with a clear fixative. 99**

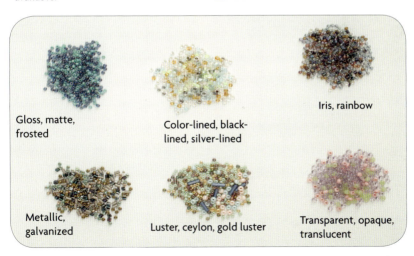

Gloss, matte, frosted

Color-lined, black-lined, silver-lined

Iris, rainbow

Metallic, galvanized

Luster, ceylon, gold luster

Transparent, opaque, translucent

22 How do I choose findings for earrings?

23 How do I use fishhooks and hoops?

24 What are threaders and chandeliers?

25 How do I use posts and clip-ons?

26 Can I make my own wires?

27 How do I choose findings for necklaces and bracelets?

28 What are spring rings and lobsters?

29 How do I use magnetic clasps?

30 Where should I use toggles, S-hooks, and barrels?

31 What is the difference between box clasps and sliders?

32 What are the standard necklace lengths, and can the length be altered?

33 What is a bail?

34 Can I make my own head and eye pins?

35 What is the difference between split and jump rings?

36 What are cord ends and cones used for?

37 What is the difference between calottes and clamshells (bead tips)?

38 How do I add beads to a watch face?

39 What are spacer bars and end bars?

40 What is the difference between crimp beads and tubular crimps?

41 Do I need crimp covers?

42 Why are wire guardians and gimp used?

43 What is a bead cap?

44 How do I use stamped filigree?

# 2

# FINDINGS

Bead shops carry a wide range of findings, i.e., components used to make jewelry in a variety of metals and styles. In this chapter, we explain the most common findings, what they are used for, and how they can be used.

# Question 22:
# How do I choose findings for earrings?

There are lots of different styles, but you do need to know whether you are making them for someone with pierced ears or not. If you are not completely certain, there are findings that will allow you to swap the earrings to make them suitable for unpierced ears. Earring findings for pierced ears come in a range of styles and materials, but if you are unsure if the person who will wear the earrings is allergic to base metals or nickel, choose sterling silver or gold. Those with fresh piercings need the same high purity, as base metals leaching into the skin can permanently discolor it.

Earring findings with a screw or clip-on mechanism are ideal if you don't have pierced ears. Whatever type of finding you choose, do consider the weight of the finished earring. Large designs and heavy stone or glass beads may well be very uncomfortable for the wearer. Day-to-day earrings may need to be quite subtle – but jewelry for a big night out can be more sensational. If you're making a gift for a specific person, think about the earrings she usually wears and try to design to suit her rather than designing for yourself.

*BELOW* Fishhooks are the most common. Posts are also popular, as are clip-ons.

# Question 23:
# How do I use fishhooks and hoops?

Fishhooks go right through the ear and hook in neatly. They come in a range of styles and materials, so it is worth checking out all the possibilities. In addition to being made from different materials, some have a hook on the back to create a closed loop, while some have a flattened front edge or integral beads. Beads are added to the eye on the front of the hook, using wire or headpins.

Drop earrings have a single bead or piece of beading attached to a fishhook. They can be very subtle or very flashy depending on the beads used, but they have fewer connections and are relatively short in comparison to dangle earrings. These may involve chains with beads, or just long strands of beads. Multiple dangle strands are particularly eye-catching but may get tangled in long hair.

Hoops range in size from loops just big enough to go around the earlobe to those that are big enough to touch the shoulder. They can be augmented with beads threaded onto the hoop itself by threading on dangles made from chain, or by creating a piece of bead weaving around the curve. It is also possible to find hoops with loops already attached, to which beads can be fixed.

*ABOVE* Lever-back hoop.

*LEFT* Endless hoop.

# Question 24:
# What are threaders and chandeliers?

Threaders are quite rare, but are very beautiful and eye-catching, and allow the wearer to be more flexible with her earrings. The earring consists of a piece of fine chain around 3 in. (8 cm) long with an eye at one end and a post at the other. The post is threaded through the piercing, and part of the chain is also taken through. Beads and other ornamentation are added to the eye. Because the chain is hanging loose, it is possible to vary the length of the earring by changing how much is pulled through the ear. Unfortunately, this also makes the earrings easier to lose – a small,

clear rubber back included with each earring prevents this.

Chandeliers are not designed to attach directly to the ear – you have to attach them to a fishhook, hoop, or post. They are essentially a shape of metal with multiple eyes or holes for attaching beads – much like crystals are hung from a chandelier. They are usually teardrop or hoop-shaped and add serious wow-factor to your jewelry. If you are creating a matching set of jewelry, you may be able to find stamped filigree components (see Question 44) to match your chandeliers.

*BELOW* Gold and silver threaders (long chains) and silver and bronze chandeliers (hoops and triangular-shaped).

# Question 25:
# How do I use posts and clip ons?

Posts are the smallest and most discrete earring finding. They either have a flat surface to which cut stones can be glued, or a metal stud and an eye to attach dangles. A post with a single, suspended semiprecious bead is a classic design and perennial favorite, but you can get much more inventive.

Try adding multiple dangles with fine chain, or adding chain and beads to the butterfly on the back of the earring. Flat-fronted posts allow you to use buttons, cabochons, or polymer-clay models. Try making your own polymer-clay flowers and beads, or look for them in your nearest local bead shop (see also Question 200).

Clip-on earrings were once very popular and can be a very thoughtful gift, as they are difficult to find. Classic clip-on backs are often quite uncomfortable, as they tend to be very tight. Try to find some that are looser, or have soft pads to protect the ear. Another solution is a screw-on finding, which can be tightened to fit. It is also possible to find hoops for non-pierced ears, and ear hooks (where the jewelry is hooked over the entire ear) and ear cuffs (a metal part-tube that slides onto the cartilage at the top of the ear).

*BELOW* A selection of clip-on (left) and post earrings (top and bottom right).

# Question 26:
# Can I make my own wires?

Yes, you can make your own wires. For ear wires, 18–22 gauge with hard or half-hard wire is common. If you are making a contemporary design and are looking for something really stylish, it is worth the effort to design and make your own. It is quite easy to shape and cut the wire using basic jewelry tools. Bend the wire around the widest part of the jaws of round-nose pliers to create the shape that goes through your ear, and then use flat-nose pliers to bend the wire at an angle if required. Make loops to attach the earring with round-nose pliers, too. To finish the wires professionally, and

to prevent damaging the earlobe, you then need to use a cup bur tool to smooth the end of the wire that goes through your ear. You can use any wire around 0.6 mm in thickness, but if there is any risk of an allergy, use sterling silver or pure silver wire. Look for hard wires, which will hold their shape more than a soft craft wire. If you are really adventurous, you can buy a chasing hammer and block to flatten the ends of the wire and half-round pliers to shape the earring wires in the most professional way.

*BELOW* Use a cup bur to remove sharp edges.

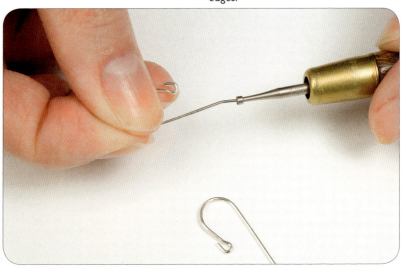

# Question 27:
# How do I choose findings for necklaces and bracelets?

As with earings, the first consideration when making a necklace or bracelet is the recipient; you must consider whether she is allergic to any metal and what style of jewelry she might like, as this will determine the type of fastening you choose. The second consideration is the beads you wish to use. You need to decide whether to use a single strand of beads or many, and whether the beads will be large or small.

The weight of beads is an important element of the design; magnetic fastenings are only suitable for lightweight jewelry, but the addition of a safety chain to bracelets or necklaces can prevent the jewelry from falling off. The style of fastening also changes, depending on the number of strands and type of stringing material.

Necklaces can have more complex findings, as they are usually fastened with both hands, but as bracelets are fastened with a single hand the findings must be simpler. Will you have a pendant? Will the design be structured or random? Necklaces can end up being quite heavy depending on the beads you use, so you will need to make sure your findings are strong enough to deal with the weight.

With a bracelet, there are different options to consider. Bracelets need to be more resistant to knocks than necklaces, and weight is a more important consideration. Like necklaces, you can either have a clasp in your bracelet, or you can have an elastic cord or use memory wire instead. If you do use a clasp, remember it will always be visible, so you may want to use a beaded loop and large bead, or button with a shank instead of a metal fastening.

Familiarize yourself with the wide variety of jewelry findings available for bracelets and necklaces in the following pages, as this will help you make more creative pieces.

# Question 28:
# What are spring rings and lobsters?

A spring ring is a basic, and generally inexpensive, fastening with a sliding spring inside a hollow, circular fastening. Spring rings usually come with a tongue (a flat oval shape with holes) that they clip into; however, you may find them easier to open and close if you substitute a jump ring. They are very secure and unobtrusive, but can be fiddly and difficult for both old and young people to fasten.

Lobster clasps, which are shaped like a lobster claw, have a swinging section that opens so that you can clip it onto a jump ring (see Question 35). Lobster clasps are much easier to open than spring rings but are not quite as secure. Both styles of fastening are suitable for both bracelets and necklaces, as they can be opened and closed with one hand. Because they are so secure, it is not necessary to use a safety chain with these fastenings.

*LEFT* Lobster clasps.

*BELOW* Spring ring.

# Question 29:
## How do I use magnetic clasps?

Magnetic clasps can be used instead of lobsters or spring rings. These elegant and sometimes surprisingly tiny fastenings contain extremely strong magnets that hold the two sides together. They were developed to allow people with poor mobility to fasten necklaces and bracelets easily. Some magnetic clasps have an additional locking system, which prevents them from pulling apart readily. Magnetic clasps are suitable for both necklaces and bracelets, but you may prefer to add a safety chain to prevent the jewelry falling off if pulled accidentally or if the fastening attaches itself to a metal object such as a chair or cabinet. The only real problem with magnetic clasps is that they are magnetic; users of pacemakers are advised not to use any form of magnetic jewelry, as it can interfere with the device. Magnetic jewelry, formed entirely from magnetic beads, is becoming more popular, too. These attractive magnetic beads are strung onto bead stringing wire and wrap around the wrist or neck to form a cuff bracelet or collar-style necklace. Some people believe that there are health benefits from wearing a magnetic bracelet, and this is an attractive alternative.

*BELOW* Magnetic clasp.

# Question 30:
# Where should I use toggles, S-hooks, and barrels?

S-hooks are necklace clasps that are very easy to fasten, and are also surprisingly thrifty – if you make all your necklaces with a ring on each end, you will only need one S-hook to fasten all of them. This is also useful if you like to mix and match your necklaces – you can easily wear two or three different matching necklaces of differing lengths without having a tangled bunch of clasps behind your neck. S-hooks should not be used with very light jewelry or on bracelets, as they come undone too easily.

Barrels, also called torpedoes or screw clasps, have two matching halves that screw together. This is a very secure means of connecting a necklace but is unsuitable for bracelets, as it is almost impossible to fully tighten the screw thread. They are also a poor choice for those with long, curly hair, as the twisting can cause the hair and necklace to get very tangled.

Toggles are essentially a T-shaped bar and a hoop of some sort. Like S-hooks, toggle clasps need a certain amount of weight to work, so they work best with heavier necklaces and bracelets. The bar is fed through the hoop lengthways, and then lies horizontally across the hoop to fasten. These fastenings come in the widest range of styles, and are particularly useful with bracelets, where the clasp is always visible. For asymmetric necklaces or lariat styles, a toggle clasp can become the central feature. The first one or two beads next to the bar have to be fairly small, as there needs to be enough play to allow the bar to pull through the hoop.

*BOTTOM LEFT S-hooks.*
*BOTTOM RIGHT Toggles. BELOW Barrels.*

# Question 31:
# What is the difference between box clasps and sliders?

Both of these are findings designed specifically for multistrand necklaces and bracelets.

Box clasps are two-piece clasps that open when you push down on the exterior lever of a wedge-shaped piece of metal, compressing it so that it slides out of an opening in the side of the box. When the wedge is pushed back in, the clasp clicks into place, holding the necklace together. Box clasps are easy to use but often do not have as much strength as lobster claw clasps (see Question 28) and can be quite heavy. They can be plain or decorative and are made in a variety of shapes and sizes, making them particularly useful for bracelets. They are traditional for multistrand pearl necklaces, adding a pretty decorative touch at the back of the neck. These fastenings come in different lengths and are most commonly found with two to six loops. Expect that, over time, the folded tab inside will break from wear.

Sliders consist of two tubes, one fitting inside the other. The tubes slot into one another and are held together by friction or a small magnet.

A less common variant has a bar on either side, allowing you to attach strands more flexibly; it is possible to attach more than one strand to each loop on a standard slider. The threads or cord are secured in each end of the fastening by squeezing the tube flat with pliers.

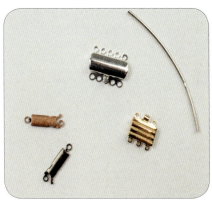

*RIGHT* The box clasps shown can be used for different numbers of strands. The slider in the top right will hold a number of fine strands, or a single thicker strand.

# Question 32:
# What are the standard necklace lengths, and can the length be altered?

Necklaces can be made any length you want. However, there are standard lengths that have become popular over the years and it is useful to know what they are, as it makes designing necklaces much easier. If you want to extend the length of a necklace or bracelet, use an extension chain. These are particularly useful when making a piece of jewelry as a gift where you might need to guess the size. You can buy extension chains, which are about 2³/₄ in. (7cm) long and have a tiny metal weight at the end, or you could make your own more decorative extension chain using a drop bead or even a bead cluster as the weight. The extension chain can then become part of the design, as it hangs down your back rather elegantly when the necklace is at its shortest length.

### Collar or choker 12–16 inches (30–41 cm)
The choker is the shortest style of necklace. It fits snugly around the neck and can have drop beads and dangles attached that hang down to soften the rather hard line cutting across the neck. A collar lies slightly lower, forming a wide, flat band that sits over the collar bone. It is a bold, luxurious style to wear.

### Princess 17–19 inches (43–48 cm)
The princess necklace is the standard length of the classic pearl necklace but it is also the perfect length for pendants, as they will sit high on the chest. The princess length is a versatile necklace that can be worn with all sorts of necklines.

### Matinee 20–24 inches (51–61 cm)
This style is traditionally worn for more informal occasions but works well with collars, suits, and dresses.

### Opera 28–34 inches (71–86 cm)
The opera necklace, which should be long enough to fall below the bust line, was popularized in the 1920s and is still often worn with long evening dresses. One style of opera necklace, called a sautoir, has a large tassel at the bottom that makes it suitable for women of all sizes, as it hangs elegantly over the bust line.

### Ropes over 45 inches (138 cm)
Long and dramatic, you can ring the changes, as the rope can be looped

or knotted more than once. Lariats are extra long ropes with both ends not joined together and are one of the most versatile styles. A lariat can have a loop and toggle fastening on each end, or a decorative tassel. The lariat can be wrapped around the neck, doubled over, or knotted, and is often worn with the ends dangling down the back.

# Question 33:
# What is a bail?

A bail is a finding that turns a bead or other object into a pendant. There are lots of different styles to suit all sorts of beads, from a donut ring to a tiny drop bead. Most are attached by slotting the bead onto one wire end and pinching the two sides together with pliers to secure.

- **Triangle bails** are just a short length of wire bent in a triangle shape with the split in the middle of the bottom edge. The triangle bail is generally used for small drop beads.
- **Standard bails** have a tensioned overlap as a closure.
- **Split loop pendant bails** have a solid loop for the cord with a split loop at the bottom. You can attach a drop bead, filigree, or dangle to the loop to make a pendant.

- **Snap-on or hinged bails** use a magnetic or spring action to stay closed.
- **Bead hanger bails** can be used like a large headpin and attach a jump ring to hang (see also Queston 163).

**Glue-fix bails**:
- **Donut bails** are used to hang large, donut-shaped beads and come in several forms. Some are glued to the top of the bead, whereas others loop through the center hole like folding bails and wire wrap bails.
- **Fold-over bails** have two decorative pads, often in the shape of leaves, which are connected with a thin strip that forms the loop for the cord when folded over.
- **Bell caps** have spider legs that are glued around any bead or object to create a pendant.
- **Flat-backed "y" bails** are glued to the back of cabochons.
- **Other** bails are variations of a loop through which you can thread a cord or chain.

# Question 34:
# Can I make my own head and eye pins?

You can make both headpins and eye pins to use in your jewelry. The eye pins will look almost identical to the bought version but, as craft wire is generally slightly softer than the wire used by manufacturers, they will handle differently. It is easier, for example, to make bead links out of homemade eye pins, as it is easier to get both loops the same size and the softer craft wire is much more malleable to create a wrapped loop. A good wire to use is 0.6 mm. It is just firm enough to hold its shape and gives a lovely delicate look to bead links. You can go up to a 0.8 mm wire; the finished result is much chunkier, which may suit some more contemporary designs. It is difficult for the hobby jewelry maker to make traditional headpins with the little flat end (you would need to use a torch to melt the wire and then flatten with an anvil), but you can easily create a decorative end that will stop beads from falling off. Decorative head pins look stunning when made up as earrings or as dangles in a necklace. Make a tiny "u" shape on the end of the wire and then, holding the "u" in round-nose pliers, wrap the wire around to begin the coil. Change to flat-nose pliers and hold the coil between the jaws. Keep wrapping the wire around a little and then moving it around until the coil is the size required. Bend the tail back to create a right angle above the coil, and then add beads and finish the dangle with a plain or wrapped loop (see Question 165).

*LEFT* Handmade eye pin dangles.

# Question 35:
# What is the difference between split and jump rings?

These two terms are often confused, as the term split ring seems to describe what is actually a jump ring. Essentially, jump rings are made by wrapping wire around a mandrel or round-nose pliers once, whereas split rings are wrapped round twice and are thus more secure. Although you can buy split rings that are as small as jump rings, split rings are generally larger and used for accessories such as key rings. If you plan to use a lot of split rings, you can buy special split ring pliers that open the rings to allow you to slot the key in. Jump rings are the most commonly used finding and come in a range of sizes and finishes. They are used in all sorts of ways such as joining chain, bead links, dangles, or fastenings. Jump rings can be used decoratively as spacers between beads. If you join several together and then string through each ring you will create a very attractive small cluster. Jump rings are also used for chain maille (see Question 168), which is an increasingly popular jewelry technique. You can make your own jump rings by wrapping wire around a mandrel and snipping each ring off in turn. Use side cutters and trim the end squarely. Consider investing in a jewelers saw if you are going to make these often (see Question 159 for more information).

*BELOW* Jump rings are single-wire circles that connect jewelry components.

*BELOW* Split rings are stronger, as the wire is wrapped around twice.

# Question 36:
# What are cord ends and cones used for?

Cord ends (also called leather crimps, ribbon ends, clamp ends, and crimp ends) are used to neaten the ends of cord, ribbon, or leather thong (see also Question 81). You slot the cord inside and bend the metal flaps in one at a time with flat-nose pliers. Cord ends have a tiny spike, which also grips the cord, but it is important to close and tighten the cord end properly. Cord ends come in a range of metals and colors and are far neater than knotting ribbon or cord to the necklace clasp.

Spring ends are a different version of cord ends – they are a stiff spring with the first loop bent upward. Clasps are attached to the upright loop with jump rings, and then the thong or cord is pushed into the spring. Once it's in place you can use flat-nose pliers to pinch the last coil tight, holding the cord in place.

Cones are much more decorative than cord and spring ends. They come in a range of sizes, materials, and styles, and cover the ends of threaded necklaces and are particularly useful for multistrand necklaces (see also Question 84). You need to choose a size of end cone that will fit snugly around the strands. Essentially, the strands are finished with loops and these can be attached to an eye pin, which is then threaded through the cone. The ends are pulled firmly up inside the cone and then a wrapped loop is formed at the top of the cone to secure the necklace strands inside and to allow you to attach the clasps.

*RIGHT* A variety of end cones and cord ends.

# Question 37:
# What is the difference between calottes and clamshells (bead tips)?

Calottes and clamshells (bead tips) look superficially the same, being two half globes connected by a hinge with a loop attached to connect to fastenings. The difference between the calotte and clamshell is that a clamshell (sometimes called a knot cup or bead tip) is hinged at the bottom, with a hole in the hinge for the thread, while calottes hinge at the side and have a hole in one cup edge. This makes the hinge stronger, but means you have to press the two sides together firmly.

When making necklaces, the first clamshell is attached to the bead string before you string the beads, so it acts like a beadstop. You knot the thread or attach a crimp to the beading wire and pass it through the hole, with the two "shells" facing toward the knot or crimp. The shells are then pressed together with the fingers or flat-nose pliers, and the necklace can be constructed. At the other end, you thread another clamshell and then attach a crimp or knot the thread, taking it down snugly into the shell with the tip of a needle as you tighten it. Once the shells are closed, you can attach the necklace fastenings to the clamshell loops to finish the piece.

With calottes, it is not necessary to attach them before creating the piece, as they can be closed over the knots once you have finished the necklace. You must make sure you close the calotte fully with pliers, or the knot may work its way out.

*LEFT* Clamshells shown on the left, calottes on the right.

# Question 38:
# How do I add beads to a watch face?

If you are making a present for someone who doesn't wear a lot of jewelry, a watch with an exquisite beaded bracelet could be an alternative gift. Watch faces are available in various styles and finishes to suit all sorts of beads and beading techniques.

There are two main types of watch faces available: those with loops to attach strings of beads or chain, and those with holes through the back of the watch face for wire or bead string. These two styles give you a huge number of options for adding beads. You can make a wide bracelet using chain-maille techniques, bead stitching, or bead loom work, or simply string some really gorgeous beads and attach through the holes or to the rings on each side of the watch face.

Watch faces with several rings or holes on each side are ideal for multistrand bracelets, and as those with holes tend to have straight sides, bead netting or bead weaving can be worked right up to the side of the watch without difficulty.

The watch fastening you choose will depend on the technique you have used to make the bracelet. Toggle fastenings are popular for bead strings, but multistrand fastenings and end bars are ideal for wider styles (see also Question 30).

*BELOW* Beaded watches are a good gift for those who do not wear much jewelry.

# Question 39:
# What are spacer bars and end bars?

Spacer bars and end bars or multi-row fasteners are generally used together to create multistrand bracelets and necklaces. End bars can have as few as two loops but more commonly have three, five, or seven. Usually, a single string of beads is attached to each loop to create a multistrand bracelet or necklace, but you can also work vertical netting between loops instead. One end bar usually has a fastener, such as a lobster clasp (see Question 28) attached to it, while the other may have an extension chain. End bars are available in several metallic finishes. A different style of end bar, which is a piece of metal folded in half with teeth along each long edge, is used for attaching findings to ribbon or bead loom work.

Spacer bars are spaced through the necklace or bracelet, holding the strands separate, and are usually sold to match the end bars. Spacer bars are particularly useful for collar-style necklaces where the strings of beads lie flat around your neck. Really striking spacers with fifteen holes can be found, but fewer holes are more common. Spacers are commonly cuboids, flat sheets, or a series of connected loops; the cuboids, in particular, can be very ornate and form an overt part of the necklace design.

*BELOW* Spacer and end bars come in lots of designs; choose one that suits the design of your piece.

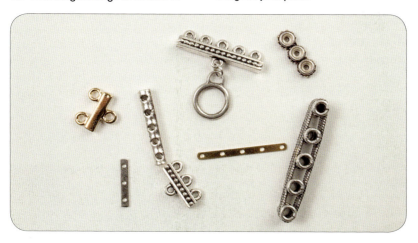

# Question 40:
# What is the difference between crimp beads and tubular crimps?

Crimp beads and tubular crimps perform the same functions but look slightly different and are secured in a different way. Crimp beads are donut-shaped metal rings, whereas tubular crimps are short metal tubes. Both types of crimps are generally used with bead stringing wire anywhere that you would use a knot with beading thread or cord (see also Question 78). So, for example, you can use crimps to space beads, to secure beading thread inside a calotte (see Question 37), or to create a loop for attaching fastenings. Crimp beads can be simply flattened with flat-nose pliers but they can look rather untidy, so they should be secured with crimp pliers (see also Question 66).

There are three sizes of crimp pliers, depending on the size of crimp you are using – micro for #1, normal for #2, and mighty for #3 crimp beads. To make things confusing, tubular crimps are a size up from crimp beads so that a #3 tube has the same internal diameter as a standard #2 crimp bead. Tubular crimps have a better finish than crimp beads and are designed to flatten into a very neat square or rectangle with flat-nose pliers. They look rather attractive when used to space beads, but you can also secure them with crimp pliers. Twisted tubular crimps, which are more decorative, should always be simply flattened.

*BELOW* These beads are specially designed to be crushed by crimping pliers.

# Question 41:
## Do I need crimp covers?

Crimp covers can be used to conceal crimped beads or tubes. To some extent, they can be used instead of calottes so that the crimp is hidden inside what looks like a small, round, metal bead. You could also use the covers to hide crimps used to space beads, so that the larger bead will have what looks like small metal beads on each side. You need large crimp pliers to secure the covers without crushing them. They are not essential but give a professional finish to necklaces and are a worthwhile additional expense for special-occasion jewelry.

Crimp covers are available in gold and silver plate as well as sterling silver. There are also textured finishes such as sparkle and ribbed, which look more like beads in jewelry. Crimp covers are usually sold pre-opened, so you simply tuck the cover over the crimp and then close using the plain circle part of the pliers. If you buy the covers closed, often called "seamed round beads," open them using an awl, which is a pointed metal tool (see Question 63). Simply push the awl gently into the closed cover to open it out, fit over the crimp, and then secure as before.

# Question 42:
## Why are wire guardians and gimp used?

Wire guardians and gimp (also known as French wire, bullion, or fancy wire) are used to prevent wear. Wire guardians are only used to protect loops of wire or thread, particularly at the ends of your work, where they are connected to fasteners. The wire guardian consists of a horseshoe shape with tubes on each end. Wire is passed through the tube, fed over the arch and through the second tube, and then the ends are crimped to complete the loop. The wire guardian protects the wire from the fastening, allowing you to use the material that best suits your project, rather than the one that best resists wear. Gimp is essentially a very long, fine spring, which is hard to crush and resists wear well. It can be used in place of the wire guardian to protect thread or to protect the inner surfaces of delicate beads such as porcelain.

# Question 43:
## What is a bead cap?

A bead cap is a decorative metal finding that is usually added to either side of beads to give an antique appearance to jewelry. They can be solid metal with a decorative finish but are most commonly made in some sort of filigree in all metallic finishes. Bead caps are readily available in a range of sizes to match bead sizes up to about 25–30 mm.

To use the bead caps, you simply string one cap on, then the bead, and then the second cap. The caps aren't glued in position but are held in position because the beads are tightly packed on the string. If the beads are spaced, the caps can be secured by knots or crimps and are particularly effective when used on a bead link as part of a rosary-style necklace.

In addition to being decorative, bead caps can be used to reduce the size of a bead hole. If a bead has a particularly large hole, the bead will sit off-center on a thin bead string, but because bead caps cup the beads and have a much smaller hole, the bead will be held centrally on the string.

*BELOW* Bead caps can be found in a multitude of styles.

# Question 44:
# How do I use stamped filigree?

As the name suggests, stamped filigree is a flat piece of metal that has been stamped with a cutter to create a decorative mesh effect. Stamped filigree was used extensively in jewelry in the 1930s and is becoming increasingly popular today. The filigree findings come in all sorts of shapes, such as rounds, squares, and ovals, that can be used as connecting elements between beads in bracelets and necklaces. Because the pieces are flat, they are ideal for bib-style necklaces.

Some stamped filigree is created in particular shapes with loops soldered in position, ready to add drop beads to make quick earrings or pendants. You can also use the filigree as a base for adding beads. The beads can be sewn onto the metal using beading thread but they are usually secured with fine wire.

If the reverse side of the filigree is going to be visible, e.g., with earrings, it is important to attach the beads as neatly as possible, working out in a circular fashion or up and down in a regular way. It is easier to use two finer wires together rather than one thicker wire, but remember to tuck any ends inside so that the sharp ends don't scratch the wearer.

*BELOW* Add in beads with wire to delicate stamped filigree for a really beautiful effect.

**45**  How do I use leather and suede cord?

**46**  How do I pick the right fabric cords?

**47**  What is the difference between multi- and monofilament thread?

**48**  Where do I use natural fiber threads?

**49**  What is illusion cord used for?

**50**  When can ribbons be used with beads?

**51**  How do I incorporate metal mesh tube in jewelry?

**52**  Where do I use elastic cord?

**53**  What are the benefits of memory wire?

**54**  How do I choose the right bead stringing wire?

**55**  Which silver wire is best?

**56**  How do I use "antique" chain?

**57**  Is copper wire a good substitute for silver?

**58**  How do I use colored wires?

**59**  What is the difference between SWG and AWG?

**60**  What is a hard wire?

# 3

# THREADS AND WIRES

This chapter covers not only threads for weaving and stitching, but also the specialist stringing materials available. It covers wires for threading beads and forming into shapes and findings as well as the benefits of different types of wire.

# Question 45:
# How do I use leather and suede cord?

Leather and suede are traditional threading materials that have been used since the very first jewelry was made and worn. Because of this long history, both leather and suede are seen as having an ethnic feel and are rarely used for formal jewelry.

The most common use of cord is to hang a pendant or small group of beads, particularly for children's jewelry. The ends are either formed into a sliding knot for round leather cord, or put into spring or cord ends when using suede, which has a rectangular cross-section (see Question 36).

Leather cord is very durable and strong and is, therefore, perfect for stringing very heavy beads and pendants. Remember that it is not necessary to make a feature of the cord unless you want a rustic feel – if you are using large stone beads and need cord to deal with the weight, you can separate the large beads with smaller metal beads rather than knots; this will completely cover the cord.

Simulated or faux suede cord comes in a wider range of colors than both real suede and leather, and the dye is more consistent. Although it is possible to buy entire reels of both leather and suede, it is more usual to buy it by the foot, in the same way as ribbon.

# Question 46:
# How do I pick the right fabric cords?

Fabric cords come in two main types – satin and wax cotton – and have different properties. Satin cord drapes beautifully, whereas wax cotton works better strung with a heavy bead or, if controlled, with knotting. Satin cord has a sheen and is ideal for special-occasion jewelry whereas waxed cotton is more often used for informal designs. Decide what the piece will be used for and what effect you are looking for, and you will find it easy to choose your cord.

**Satin cord** is usually made from rayon or nylon but can be made from silk. Rayon cord is trademarked rattail – nylon cord is occasionally sold as "rat-tail."

**Rayon satin cord** comes in more than 70 colors in three sizes:

**Petite #0** is called bugtail or petite rattail and is approximately 1 mm–1.4 mm; lightweight #1 (mousetail or lightweight rattail) is approximately 1.5 mm– 1.9 mm; heavyweight #2 (rattail or heavyweight rattail) is approximately 2 mm or slightly more.

**Rayon cord** frays badly, but treating the ends with glue or fray check will help to prevent it. Nylon cord comes in fewer colors and is most often found in 2 mm thickness. This cord can be sealed at the end using a flame. Both satin cords are silky and soft and make attractive formal jewelry, but tend to catch and wear when worn every day.

**Waxed cotton** thread is much more durable than satin and is far thinner – 1 or 2 mm are the most popular sizes. It comes in a huge range of colors and can be threaded without a needle because it is fairly stiff and doesn't fray. Wax cotton is easy to knot, and you can create beautiful effects by knotting more than one color together.

*FAR LEFT* Suede cord.
*LEFT* Waxed cotton cord.
*RIGHT* Satin cord.

# Question 47:
# What is the difference between multi- and monofilament thread?

Monofilament is a thread that is formed from a single fiber whereas multifilament has lots of fine strands lying parallel, twisted, or woven (braided) together. Multifilaments tend to be softer and have more of a "fabric" feel but they are prone to wear, making them look fuzzy, or even break, especially when used with sharp-edged beads such as bugles. A thread conditioner or pre-waxed threads such as K-O help prevent this. Monofilament threads made from nylon, such as fishing line, used to be used for jewelry making but have been superceded by better quality braided threads with superior drape, such as Fireline and Dandyline. Clear nylon monofilaments are now used for illusion necklaces, where the threads look almost invisible and the beads appear to float (see also Question 85). Some monofilaments are stretchy and ideal for making bracelets without a fastening.

*BELOW* Monofilament thread is shown on the right.

# Question 48:
# Where do I use natural fiber threads?

Threads are either made from synthetic, manmade, or natural fibers. Synthetic threads, such polyester and nylon, are manufactured; manmade are recycled, usually cellulose-based to make rayon; and natural fibers, such as wool, cotton, and silk, are harvested. All these fibers have different qualities and handling properties. Standard cotton should be avoided in beadwork, as it has a tendency to disintegrate over time with mildew, but wax cotton is a fantastic natural thread that is available in a wide range of colors and can be used for all sorts of jewelry. It is ideal for knotting techniques such as macramé.

Hemp or linen threads are a great natural alternative to beading wire.

They come in various colors and thicknesses, and are frequently used with more natural beads such as shells, bone, and varnished wood.

Traditionally, pearl necklaces were strung with silk; a knot was tied between each bead to hold them apart and prevent the luster from being knocked off the precious gems. Silk thread knots beautifully and has a lovely sheen. It is now available in very bright modern colors and can be teamed with colored glass pearls to create a beautiful contemporary style. Look for silk thread sold with an integral needle – this allows you to use much thicker thread, as it does not have to be doubled through the needle.

*BELOW* Silk thread.

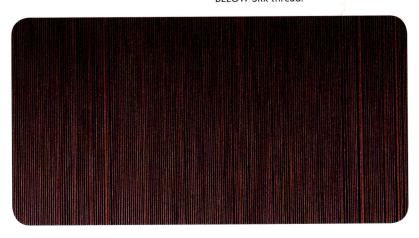

# Question 49:
## What is illusion cord used for?

Illusion cord is a monofilament most often sold clear, rather than colored. This is because it is primarily used in applications where the thread is almost invisible. There are two main applications for illusion cord: illusion or "floating" necklaces, and bead weaving or pulled-thread loom work.

Floating necklaces use multiple strands of illusion cord with beads scattered along them. The beads are usually held in place with either glue or crimps, in such a way that they look almost as if they are floating above the skin.

Most bead weaving is worked so closely that the thread is hidden between the beads almost entirely. However, when working a right-angle weave, chain stitch, or bead motifs, the threads are more visible. Using a thin illusion cord means the threads are almost entirely invisible, and this is particularly useful when working with transparent beads or crystals, as the thread is not visible within the beads and does not distort the colors. Illusion cord is also stiffer than multifilament bead threads, and so 3-D bead motifs will hold their shape and are less likely to be floppy.

*BELOW* A "floating" necklace.

# Question 50:
# When can ribbons be used with beads?

Ribbons are very attractive when included in necklaces, and you should experiment with substituting them for standard threading materials as often as possible. Matt beads can be contrasted with satin ribbon, while gloss beads can be enhanced with organza ribbon. Ribbon can be substituted for leather cord when hanging a pendant, or a thick velvet ribbon can be used to create a choker.

When you use striped ribbons for knot work, the colors swirl through the knots. It is more difficult to knot ribbon than thread or cord, but the effects that can be achieved make it worth the trouble (see Questions 90 and 91). You can experiment with ribbons, adding more than one ribbon to create a multithread necklace, and using multiple colors and textures. Substitute strips of torn fabric to create a gypsy look or use scrap-booking fibers for a funkier feel. Use cones and bar crimp ends to secure the ribbons to the fastening (see Question 36).

*BELOW* Necklace with ribbon.

# Question 51:
# How do I incorporate metal mesh tube in jewelry?

Metal mesh tube is the most flexible of all the stringing materials. It is commonly used like ribbon, threading large hole beads onto it, or with beads inside the mesh.

Tubular ribbon is woven from brass, copper, or aluminium, and is coated in enamel and lacquered to prevent color changes. It is sold by the foot in the same way as ribbon, in various widths and a multitude of colors; some also have different strands woven through to create different patterns and textures.

Because the mesh is waterproof, heat resistant, and nickel-free, it does not cause allergic reactions and can even be baked in an oven, so polymer clay can be worked into it.

Used as a ribbon to support a pendant, the mesh has a glittery texture like reptile scales. It is equally beautiful when used as a tube with beads of various sizes and shapes inside it to create a stunning bangle, or it can be fluffed out to nearly three times its original size, creating beautiful swirls and waves when used over a jewelry wire. Simple necklaces that alternate beads inside and outside the mesh are perhaps the most striking use of mesh tube.

# Question 52:
# Where do I use elastic cord?

Jewelry for young children should always be strung on elastic, as it is less likely to snap and send beads across your floor. It can be washed easily, fits large and small children, and it is easy to take on and off.

Elastic cord is also perfect for adult bangles where a clasp would be too fussy or would detract from the beads used. Those with metal allergies can use elastic as an alternative to clasps in necklaces, as long as the jewelry is entirely beaded.

Thin elastic can be doubled up if you are struggling to thread thicker elastic through your beads, and you can use twisted wire needle to thread the elastic. Avoid weighty beads, as they will simply stretch the elastic, leaving unsightly gaps; plastic or wooden beads should be used rather than large numbers of semiprecious stones. Elastic should be knotted using a square knot (see Question 91), and then sealed with superglue before trimming the ends. Pull the elastic around until the knot is hidden inside a bead with a large hole. It is advisable to lay the necklace or bangle flat before tying the ends – this means that you will not inadvertently overstretch the elastic.

# Question 53:
# What are the benefits of memory wire?

Memory wire is very hard wire that is pre-shaped in a circle. It holds its shape, and because of this, it can be used to form jewelry with no clasps. Memory wire is perfect for children and those with mobility problems, and is good to use when you're not sure of sizes.

Bracelets can be easily formed from a spiral of memory wire with beads threaded on and secured with crimps. The spiral will move apart to accommodate your hand sliding in, and then snap back into shape to prevent it from falling off. Necklaces made of memory wire should be formed from a single loop – spirals are not as comfortable to wear

around your neck and are far more difficult to put on.

You can buy memory wire as a long coil in necklace, bracelet, or ring diameter, but you will need heavy-duty wire cutters, as ordinary jewelers cutters will be damaged by the extreme hardness of the wire. If you are only making one or two pieces, it is possible to buy memory wire that is already cut to length. You can bend the ends of the wire over to stop the beads from falling off or buy ball ends that are glued in position (see also Question 83).

*BELOW* Memory wire comes in a number of different sizes.

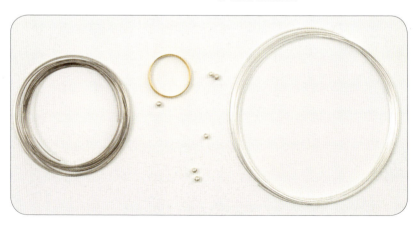

# Question 54:
# How do I choose the right bead stringing wire?

Bead stringing wire is made from strands of stainless steel inside a nylon coating; this gives it the soft feel of thread while retaining the strength of steel. Stringing wire is sold by the number of steel strands and the diameter of the wire. The number of strands does not affect the diameter; 0.30 mm wire can be found with 49 very slender strands, or 7 much thicker ones.

The strand number gives the level of flexibility in the wire – 49 strand is the most flexible and most expensive wire, which forms a lovely curve around the wearer even when using very light beads. 7 strand wire tends to coil up unless very heavy beads are used, and is more easily damaged, either kinking or abrading with frequent use.

Bead stringing wire should always be chosen to fill as much of the bead holes as possible. When the wire holds the bead closely, it is less likely to wear it away.

To choose the right wire, pick the diameter and color that best suits your beads, then select the drape; consider the weight of the beads you will be using and how much flexibility you require. 19 strand wire is a good all-purpose drape, but if you are looking for extreme flexibility, you will need a 49 strand wire; likewise, if you need a stiffer effect, choose a 7 strand wire. Bead stringing wire is available in a wide range of colors and metallic finishes as well as precious metals for very special pieces.

- Seed beads – diameter is 0.25 mm
- Large hole glass or metal beads – diameter is 0.91 mm
- General purpose use – diameter is 0.46 mm or 0.38 mm

# Question 55:
# Which silver wire is best?

Silver wires, including head pins and eye pins, are either plated, sterling silver, or fine silver. For most jewelry, silver-plated wire, usually with a copper core can be used. One disadvantage of plated wire is that the plating can wear off in constant use, or you can end up removing the plating with repeated cleaning. You can buy non-tarnish wire, which is less likely to discolor over time, but it is more expensive. Plated wires are available in a range of thicknesses and in soft to hard metals.  Real silver wire is much more expensive and generally used only for really special pieces or to make jewelry that requires soldering or shaping with a chasing hammer and block. Fine silver is 99.9 percent pure, and sterling silver is 92.5 percent pure, and both are about ten times more expensive than silver plate. Silver wire is available in round and square shapes. Fine silver is softer than sterling silver but extremely malleable, so you can get very thin wires – 0.03 mm is even thinner than human hair. If you want to make your own earring wires, it is worth buying sterling silver wire rather than silver plate, and if you are allergic to nickel, use fine silver instead.

*BELOW LEFT* Silver-plated wire.
*BELOW RIGHT*  Fine silver wire.

# Question 56:
# How do I use "antique" chain?

Antique-style chains are widely available. Made in copper, silver, or gold, they are generally darker and duller than non-antique chains of the same color. Antique chains give jewelry a lovely vintage feel and are gorgeous against most skin colors because of their warmer tones.

The only downside to using antique chains is that it is often difficult to find wire to match – and the choice of findings may also be restricted. You can solve this problem in two ways: first, you can use antique headpins with the heads cut off to provide short lengths of wire for bead links and fastenings; and second, you can apply your own patina to findings or lengths of wire.

Bottled patinas are available for a range of metals, and good results can be obtained with them, though you may find it too much effort unless you have a lot of wire and findings to be antiqued to achieve a particular effect.

## EXPERT TIP

❝ You can antique silver, copper, or brass wire by submerging it in a bowl of hot water with a few drops of liver of sulfur. Once it has been soaked for a few minutes, rinse in lukewarm water and pat dry. Leave overnight and then polish with steel wool and a soft cloth. It is possible to use this method on whole bracelets and necklaces, as long as the beads are not polymer clay, bone, or ivory (spot test other natural beads or beads with coatings). ❞

# Question 57:
# Is copper wire a good substitute for silver?

Sterling silver wire is the brightest, most expensive wire available for making jewelry. It is perfect for luxury jewelry, evening wear, and earrings (as it is less likely to cause allergies). For everyday wear, though, sterling silver may be an overly expensive option.

Copper wire is a good substitute for sterling silver, as it is widely available and easily workable. It is cheap enough to practice with, but at the same time is very attractive – particularly when coiling or wrapping beads, as this will create a very individual and unique look.

The other big advantage of using copper and silver is that the scrap can be easily sorted – pure wire scrap can be melted down and recycled, and you are likely to be able to sell your scrap sterling silver. Another alternative to silver is aluminium – this is very soft, so it can be textured, coiled, woven, or knitted. It is also possible to get very thick gauges that can be used to create cuff-style jewelry.

*BELOW* Bead decoration piece with ribbon, made using copper wire. Pendant with chain made from copper wire.

# Question 58:
# How do I use colored wires?

Colored wire is enameled, so the main issue you will find when using it is the color being scratched or flaked off. The best way to prevent color damage is to buy good-quality enameled wire, as this is far less likely to flake. Obviously, it is a good idea to work enameled metal as little as possible – hammering, in particular, is likely to damage the finish. It is important to use smooth pliers rather than serrated pliers, which will scratch the surface. Plastic jaw pliers are also suitable.

Colored wire is particularly well suited to wire jig work and chain maille; these add a unique touch to your jewelry and are very eye-catching. A simple and attractive use of colored wire is to make twisted-wire jump rings: twisting wire tightly and then forming the twist into a coil and cutting it into separate rings. Each ring should then be lightly hammered to fuse the separate wires.

Use two thin, colored wires to create beautiful crochet or knitting; wire sold as crochet wire is usually 0.315 mm in diameter and is particularly soft so that it doesn't snap easily. This is a problem with thinner wires, but if you combine the two thicknesses, you will have a lovely texture and the work will be both strong and supple.

*BELOW* An assortment of colored wires.

# Question 59:
# What is the difference between SWG and AWG?

Both of these are measurements of wire thickness. AWG stands for American Wire Gauge, and SWG stands for Standard Wire Gauge. As you can see from the table below, the sizes cover a wide range, from 0.025 mm to 4 mm thickness, so it is important to be sure you are buying the correct width, as a mistake will lead to it not fitting through your beads. The higher the AWG or SWG, the thinner the wire.

| mm | AWG | SWG | mm | AWG | SWG | mm | AWG | SWG |
|------|-----|-----|-------|-----|-----|-------|-----|-----|
| 4 | | 8 | 0.71 | | 22 | 0.212 | | 35 |
| 3.25 | | 10 | 0.7 | 21 | | 0.2 | 32 | 36 |
| 3 | | 11 | 0.63 | | 23 | 0.17 | | 37 |
| 2.65 | | 12 | 0.6 | 22 | | 0.15 | 34 | 38 |
| 2.36 | | 13 | 0.56 | | 24 | 0.132 | | 39 |
| 2 | 12 | 14 | 0.5 | 24 | 25 | 0.125 | | 40 |
| 1.8 | | 15 | 0.45 | | 26 | 0.112 | | 41 |
| 1.6 | | 16 | 0.4 | 26 | 27 | 0.1 | 38 | 42 |
| 1.5 | 14 | | 0.375 | | 28 | 0.09 | | 43 |
| 1.4 | | 17 | 0.315 | | 30 | 0.08 | | 44 |
| 1.25 | | 18 | 0.3 | 28 | | 0.071 | | 45 |
| 1.2 | 16 | | 0.28 | | 31 | 0.06 | | 46 |
| 1 | 18 | 19 | 0.265 | | 32 | 0.05 | | 47 |
| 0.9 | 19 | 20 | 0.25 | 30 | 33 | 0.04 | | 48 |
| 0.8 | 20 | 21 | 0.236 | | 34 | 0.025 | | 50 |

# Question 60:
# What is a hard wire?

There are three common types of wire: soft, half-hard, and hard. A hard wire is perfect for making your own clasps and weight-bearing components. It is stiff and strong enough to keep its shape under strain, but the stiffness makes it more difficult to work. This type of wire is not suitable for wrapping techniques, especially when using delicate beads, as the force required to shape it is likely to damage them. Hard wire is more brittle than soft wire, and will become weaker the more it is worked, so it is important to plan carefully before beginning to work the wire – if it is worked too much, it will snap.

Soft wires are the opposite of hard wires. They are unsuitable for making weight-bearing components and clasps, as they will quickly deform or pull apart. Soft wire is easy to twist and wrap, and can be hammered to create texture. It is ideal for knitting and crochet, and can be formed into springs for decoration, used to make spiral or wrapped beads, or twisted together to create beautiful wire ropes.

Half-hard wire falls in the middle and is a good all-around choice. However, if you want to really work the wire, buy soft wire; likewise, if you want to create your own findings, buy a specialist hard wire.

*BELOW* A close-up shot of hard wire.

**61** Are beading mats, boards, and scoops essential?

**62** What are stoppers?

**63** What is the difference between reamers and awls?

**64** How do I measure my jewelry?

**65** What is the best way to cut loose threads?

**66** Do I need to use crimping pliers?

**67** Why do I need files and cup burs?

**68** Are conditioners and thread zappers essential for bead stitching?

**69** How do I properly use wire cutters?

**70** What types of flat-nose pliers are available?

**71** How do I choose the right round-nose pliers?

**72** What is the best way to store my beads?

**73** How do I choose and store needles?

**74** When will tapestry and other blunt needles be useful?

**75** What are the benefits of big-eye and twisted-wire needles?

**76** What is a bead loom?

# 4

# TOOLS AND EQUIPMENT

Jewelry making requires two pairs of pliers and some wire cutters; weaving, threading, and looming require needles and sharp scissors. These tools and other equipment are discussed here.

# Question 61:
## Are beading mats, boards, and scoops essential?

While it is possible to bead without any of these, they do make life much easier. Some form of mat is necessary for any beadwork, as it prevents the beads from rolling away or being knocked onto the floor. Many beginners use a piece of leather turned suede-side up or a square of felt, but your needle will get trapped in the felt fibers, especially when picking up seed beads. A proper microfiber bead mat is inexpensive and much easier to use; the fibers in the short pile hold the beads still and allow you to pick them up easily onto wire or a needle.

Beading boards are used to design necklaces before stringing. They are most often made of flocked plastic to prevent beads from rolling, and have grooves to lay out single or multiple strands of beads. Measurements are given around the center and edge of the board to allow you to make a specific length of necklace. You can put beads and findings into the storage sections on the board, which allows you to quickly shuffle beads and try out different combinations.

Bead scoops come in all sorts of sizes and shapes, and they are not an essential. However, once you have one, you will wonder what you ever did without it! The scoop allows you to pick up beads from your work surface and put them back into their container quickly and easily. They are particularly useful for bead looming and weaving, which use large numbers of seed beads in multiple colors at the same time.

*BELOW* Your bead board, scoops, and beading mat.

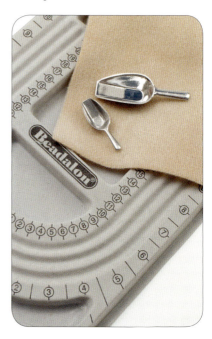

# Question 62:
# What are stoppers?

A stopper is a bead or spring that prevents beads from coming off thread or wire as you work and is essential when bead stringing – at some point your work is going to slither off the table, and if the end of the cord is not properly secured, the beads will pour all over the floor. Necklaces that use clamshells at the ends will not need a stopper, and it is possible to simply put a large knot in threads or cords (see Question 37).

Often when bead weaving, particularly the peyote stitch, you can use a stopper bead to hold the initial beads. Use a different color bead so that it can be removed later, and simply take the thread back through the bead twice to hold it in place and begin beading.

Alternatively, you can use a small bead-stopper spring, which is also ideal for bead stringing wire. These brilliant little gizmos are springs with the end coils bent back; when pressed toward one another, the coils spread apart and a thread or wire can be placed between them. The spring can be easily moved up and down the thread, and if you have multiple springs, you can easily put your work down, work on more than one strand, or try out a necklace without worrying about losing beads. A quick alternative to a proper bead spring is a paper clip, but this is less secure and it is more difficult to create tension in your work.

*BELOW* Bead stopper springs come in different sizes for different thicknesses of cords and wires.

# Question 63:
# What is the difference between reamers and awls?

Bead reamers and awls look superficially similar, but are used for very different things. The reamer will have a number of differently sized heads that are encrusted with fine diamond powder. It is primarily used for smoothing the edges of beads that would otherwise damage the stringing material. It can also be used to enlarge or remove partial blockages in bead holes.

Use the reamer under running water, as this will wash away the dust and prevent the bead from getting blocked up. This is particularly important when you are working with organic beads as the fine dust created can be harmful.

An awl is essentially a pointed stick with a very smooth working surface. It can be used when knotting to site overhand knots. Once you have tied your knot loosely, slip the point of the awl into the knot and gently slide it down to where you want the knot to be. Holding the awl firmly, pull the knot tight and then remove the awl to leave the knot in the correct position. You can use a large tapestry needle instead. Awls can also be used to open split beads with crimp covers and to make large holes or texture patterns in polymer clay beads.

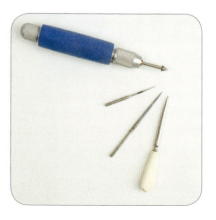

*RIGHT  Blue handle:* The reamer has a number of ends. These fit inside the handle of the tool when not in use. *White handle:* This vintage awl is beautiful and still usable today.

# Question 64:
# How do I measure my jewelry?

The most obvious way of measuring jewelry, which everyone uses when they buy it, is to try it on. This is not always practical when making jewelry, although it is likely that you will try most pieces on as a final check.

When you are using a beading board (see Question 61), you will be able to measure the length on the board; remember to add the length of your fastenings and crimps if you are using them. Use a piece of the stringing material (with any pendant you are using threaded on) held at the right length to see where it lies. Always look in the mirror, not down at your own chest, to see the fit.

Bead loom work can be trickier. Measure around your wrist with a tape measure and then measure a section of the work (for example, ten rows) and work out how many rows you will need to create your bracelet. Remember to subtract the length of your findings.

Strung bracelets can be measured in three ways: items you are making for yourself can be wrapped around your wrist; you can measure them lying flat with a tape measure; or you can measure the wearable length using an EZ sizer. Wearable length differs from flat length due to the diameter of the beads used. A seed bead bracelet has almost the same wearable and flat lengths because the beads are so narrow. A bracelet made of 1 in. (2.5 cm) diameter beads with the same flat length as the seed bead bracelet has much less wearable diameter than the seed bead bracelet when fastened, because half of each bead is taking up the space that should be occupied by your wrist.

*LEFT* Using an EZ sizer will help you make sure that your jewelry fits the intended wearer. You can keep track of the size of the project as you work.

# Question 65:
# What is the best way to cut loose threads?

The best way to cut loose threads is to do so carefully! It is all too easy to cut too close to knots, allowing them to unravel. Long-bladed scissors are unwieldy and carry the risk of accidentally cutting more than one part of your work.

The best scissors for jewelry work are small with very sharp, narrow blades. These will allow you to make precision cuts close to your work. These should never be used for cutting thick cord or any wires, as it can loosen the rivet or will damage the blades.

Thread snips are spring loaded and are easy to pick up and cut quickly. Because you hold the snips close to the blades, you have greater control than with scissors, and so they are ideal for trimming threads close to the work and avoiding costly mistakes. Thread snips are also ideal for cutting lengths of thread from a reel but are not so good for ribbon or cord; use larger shears for those materials. For bead weaving and stitching, a thread zapper can be useful (see Question 68).

*BELOW* Small scissors, best for cutting loose threads near knots with precision.

*BELOW* Thread snips. The pointy tips on these tools make them more effective at cutting ribbon and cord.

# Question 66:
# Do I need to use crimping pliers?

Crimping pliers are not necessary to work with tubular crimps, as they are flattened with flat-nose pliers to create a neat square or rectangle. Crimp beads can be flattened with flat-nose pliers, but they are designed to be secured onto wire using crimping pliers. Crimping pliers are available in three sizes, and it is essential to match the crimp to the size of tool. Normal pliers are used for size 2 crimp beads, with micro and mighty tools for sizes 1 and 3, respectively.

Crimping pliers have two sets of notches in the jaws. Closest to the hinge is a semicircular lower notch with a double notch above; the wire and crimp is first placed in this notch, where it is squashed into a crescent shape. The notches closest to the end of the pliers are both semicircular, and are used to fold the cresent shape in half. The finished crimp is a rounded shape, which is half the size of a crimp flattened with ordinary pliers. When used with seed beads, a properly folded crimp is almost indistinguishable.

*BELOW* Crimps are often used to create small loops in beading wire.

# Question 67:
# Why do I need files and cup burs?

However you cut wires, the ends are always sharp. When you are working with thin wires, knitting, or crocheting, the ends are usually tucked inside the work or into findings to keep the edges away from the skin.

When working with thicker wires, it is not always practical to just hide the ends of your work. You can smooth rough edges using an emery board or special jewelry files.

If you make your own ear wires, a cup bur will be indispensable – it is essentially a tiny cup-shaped file on the end of a handle. By spinning the wire in the cup bur, you can round off the whole tip of the wire, removing all of the rough edges (see also Question 26).

*RIGHT* It is possible to get cup burs in different sizes for different thicknesses of wire.

# Question 68:
# Are conditioners and thread zappers essential for bead stitching?

In reality, all you need for bead stitching is a needle and thread, small scissors, and the beads, but if you are doing a lot of tightly packed bead stitching and looking for a professional finish, conditioners and thread zappers can be invaluable.

Conditioners coat the thread with a fine layer of wax or a wax substitute and stop the thread from tangling as you stitch. Originally, beeswax was used and then substitutes like Thread Heaven and more recently microcrystalline wax were developed, which are far superior. Conditioners can be a little controversial, as some beaders use them all the time but others not at all. Some beaders who work tight geometric shapes in bead stitches swear by conditioner, as the wax prevents the thread from slipping

back through the bead resulting in a much tighter stitch.

To apply conditioner, tuck the thread under your index finger on the top of the conditioner and then pull the thread through. Pull the thread a couple of times between your index finger and thumb to distribute and evenly coat the thread. If applying wax to Fireline, a pre-waxed braided bead thread, pull the thread through a paper tissue to remove any excess oil first.

A thread zapper is a battery-operated tool that cuts and seals the end of threads by singeing or melting, depending on whether the thread is a synthetic or natural fiber. The fine tip of the tool easily gets between tiny beads so that those annoying tiny tails of thread that can mar a piece of bead work are instantly removed (see also Question 95).

*LEFT* The thread zapper is an easy way to deal with thread ends.

# Question 69:
# How do I properly use wire cutters?

Wire cutters for jewelry have a flat side and an indented side to the jaws. The indented side cuts the end of the wire in a "v" shape, whereas the flat side cuts the wire straight. It doesn't really matter how you hold the pliers for cutting a length of wire if it is going to be left as a tail, but when trimming wire close to the work, for example, when trimming a wrapped loop or making jump rings, it is essential to cut with the flat side closest to it. If you are making jump rings, the wire end left on the spiral of wire will have a "v" shape end after cutting a jump ring; you do need to flip the pliers and trim the end squarely so you are ready to cut the next ring.

You should consider safety when cutting with wire cutters, especially when cutting off tiny ends. If you turn the cutters and wire so that any tiny pieces will shoot off onto the beading mat, it is less likely to cause an injury. If cutting thicker wires, you can get tiny cuts on your hands from the sharp slithers of wire. Wire cutters are one tool that you should spend money on. The more expensive tools with a spring action to open the blades and large padded handles are so much easier to use than basic wire cutters. You will find that a higher quality tool cuts a lot better and you will wonder why you didn't think to buy one sooner.

*BELOW* Flip the wire cutters over to trim an end flush.

# Question 70:
# What types of flat-nose pliers are available?

There are four types of flat-nose pliers, but only one, the snipe or chain-nose pliers, is an essential tool for everyday work. You will only need one set of flat-nose pliers to hold wire while you bend it, but two are ideal for opening jump rings and essential for chain maille. You can get by using your round-nose pliers in one hand and flat-nose in the other. Choose pliers with fine or no serrations on the jaws so that any damage to the wire is minimal. You can wrap serrated pliers with masking tape to protect the wire.

• Standard flat-nose pliers have flat jaws that are the same width all along their length. They can be used for both crimping and holding wire firmly, and are a good working tool.

• Chain-nose or snipe-nose pliers are flat-nose pliers with tapering jaws. The outside of the jaws is sometimes domed, which is useful for bending wire to make earring wires and S-hooks. These pliers can be used in the same way as flat-nose pliers, but the added advantage is that they can fit into smaller gaps.

• Bent-nose pliers are a variant of chain-nose pliers. The tips are bent to one side, allowing you to get them into tricky places to hold your work and bend wire.

• Nylon-jawed pliers have a thick, nylon coating on the jaws, making them ideal for working with very soft aluminium wires. Kinked or bent wires can be straightened by holding them tightly with another pair of pliers, and pulling the nylon-jawed pliers under tension along the length of the wire.

*LEFT* Flat-nose pliers are an essential tool in beading.

# Question 71:
## How do I choose the right round-nose pliers?

There are four main types of round-nose pliers, which all have cone-shaped jaws. Round-nose pliers, an essential tool for jewelry making, are used to create loops in wire, allowing you to create eye pins, bead links, and jump rings. You also use round-nose pliers to create a coil in wire. Begin with a tiny "u" shape rather than a loop to make a more even, circular shape.

• Standard round-nose pliers have cone-shaped ends that taper uniformly. By holding the wire at different points you can create larger and smaller loops.

• Three-step pliers have one jaw that has three different sized steps down the tapered jaw, making it easy to create identically sized loops over and over again.

• Rosary pliers have integrated cutters; they are called "rosary" because they enable you to create rosary units with only one pair of pliers.

• Round-nose nylon pliers can be used to work either very soft aluminium wires without damaging them, or to straighten wire.

*BELOW* Round-nose pliers.

# Question 72:
# What is the best way to store my beads?

In an ideal world, all beads would be sold in the same shape and sized container, with easily opened lids. Unfortunately, beads come in all kinds of containers and bags, which are often unsuitable for repeated opening and closing.

You need to come up with a cataloguing system that suits you and your beads. If you have a lot of large beads, you will be able to store them in clear plastic bags in boxes or drawers. You may choose to store them by color, material, or size, depending on how you design your jewelry.

Seed beads can be moved into specialist stacking jars, or, if sold in tubes, can easily be stored in them. Keep empty tubes to store future purchases.

However you decide to store your beads, the most important thing is to make sure you mark the new container with the bead details such as size, color, code number, and where you bought them; otherwise you may be unable to match them at a future date.

*BELOW* Find an easy way to catalogue and store your beads.

# Question 73:
## How do I choose and store needles?

Specialist needles are created for every aspect of beadwork, and all have a thin eye relative to the needle so that they can pass through bead holes. Beading needles are available in a range of lengths: extra long for bead loom weaving, long for bead stitching, and short for embroidery, although it is personal preference whether you like a long or medium needle. Long beading needles are prone to bend and break easily, so you will need to keep a good supply. As a general guide, pick a needle that is at least one size smaller than the bead, but if you are going to be passing the needle through the bead several times, as in bead weaving, you may need to choose a thinner needle. Size 10 beading needles are a good standard, ideal for size 11 seed beads. For techniques like spiral cords, you can use the finer size 13 needle. You may find it easier to thread needles if you pick one that matches your thread; beading needles have rectangular holes, which are well shaped for multifilament threads, whereas round, twisted threads will fit more easily through the round eye of a sharp sewing needle. You can store short needles in a pin cushion, but a needle pod prevents longer, finer needles from getting bent.

*BELOW* A selection of needles of different lengths and needle pods.

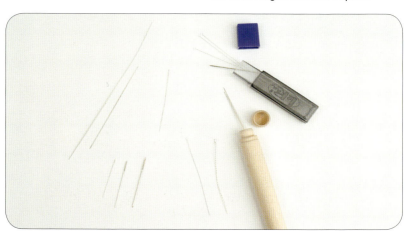

# Question 74:
# When will tapestry and other blunt needles be useful?

Tapestry needles have a large eye and are usually used for embroidery on evenweave fabric. These needles are particularly useful for threading beads onto yarn when knitting or crocheting with beads. Satin cords and waxed cotton can both be threaded through large-hole beads using a tapestry needle.

Tapestry needles can be used instead of an awl to create knots, and can also be handy to unpick a knot in the wrong place.

Blunt needles are also useful when working on the bead loom (see Question 76) – particularly when using the drawn-thread method – as they prevent you from accidentally piercing the warp threads. You can blunt the tip of a beading needle by rubbing it against fine sandpaper or an emery board.

*LEFT* Tapestry needles are useful when knitting or crocheting with beads.

# Question 75:
# What are the benefits of big-eye and twisted-wire needles?

Big-eye needles are made by soldering two very thin needles together at the ends. This creates a long, double-pointed needle with an eye almost the length of the needle. The big-eye needle can, therefore, be used to thread thicker yarns and fibers, and is particularly useful for threading ribbon. The needles are quite fragile and can easily bend out of shape. Handle carefully and store in a container rather than a pin cushion because of the double point.

Twisted-wire needles are created by twisting a thin wire tightly, leaving a round eye at the top. Ready-made twisted needles have the point soldered and sharpened. This needle is specially designed for beads with very small holes or for threading beads onto yarn. The round eye is very easy to thread but collapses as it is pulled through the beads. It is perfect for on-and-off loom work, or for stringing seed beads. You can make your own wire needles by folding thin wire in half over the jaws of round-nose pliers, then twisting the tails together. Trim the end to make a neat point.

*BELOW* Twisted-wire needles and other needles with large eyes are extremely easy to thread.

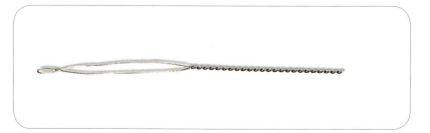

# Question 76:
# What is a bead loom?

A bead loom is a piece of equipment for weaving beads into bands or panels. The weaving can be done on any firm structure that will hold your warp threads securely while you weave through them, but as the warp threads must stay parallel and taut, it is a good idea to buy an inexpensive loom to begin.

Metal looms are made of bent wire that has a spring at each end to hold the threads parallel, and two rollers to keep the work taut. You can roll the work forward to make a longer strip.

Wooden looms are more solid, with grooves to hold the threads, and usually allow you to work a wider piece than a standard metal loom. The length can usually be adjusted by inserting longer dowels between the end panels.

Small acrylic looms are useful for creating seamless tubes; they are usually set up with a single warp thread. Acrylic looms can be found either as U-shapes or circular tubes and, as they are clear, a pattern can be taped inside for you to follow.

When choosing a bead loom, think about what sort of beading you want to do and look for one that you will find comfortable to use.

*RIGHT* Wooden and acrylic looms.

**77** How do I design strung necklaces?

**78** How is crimping used in a necklace?

**79** When is bead stringing wire useful?

**80** What is gimp and how do I use it?

**81** How are cord necklaces created and finished?

**82** Do ribbon and metal mesh ribbons need different techniques?

**83** How do I string beads onto memory wire?

**84** How do I design a multistrand necklace?

**85** What is a floating necklace?

**86** How do I create a sliding knot fastening?

**87** How do I make an overhand knot?

**88** How do I tie a reef (square) knot?

**89** What other knots are useful?

**90** How do I tie a half-knot twist?

**91** How do I tie a square-flat knot?

# 5

# STRINGING AND KNOTTING

Stringing beads is the simplest way to create jewelry; children begin making jewelry in this way. In this chapter, techniques and materials that can be used to refine and improve the design and quality of your work are described.

# Question 77:
# How do I design strung necklaces?

The first thing to decide is if you are going to have a focal point. The focal point is usually in the center, either on the string or below it, hung as a pendant or cluster of large beads. When you make an asymmetric necklace with the focal point to one side, it is called a station. This can be particularly attractive when you use a flat piece next to the collar bone.

When you design jewelry, you will find that the beads fall into three categories. The primary beads are the main focus, and are usually more expensive than the rest. Secondary beads frame the primary beads and enhance their effect. The tertiary beads are those you use to fill in the gaps. Generally, the tertiary beads are less expensive because you will need more of them.

If you use a bead board (see Question 61), you can lay out your primary beads, then add secondary beads and tertiary beads to fill in the gaps. Using the bead board allows you to rearrange your beads easily and experiment with different focal points, colors, and lengths.

*BELOW* Arranging the primary, secondary, and tertiary beads on a bead board.

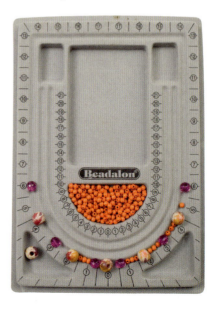

# Question 78:
# How is crimping used in a necklace?

Crimps can be used in a couple of ways: to secure beads in a particular position or to secure loops. Crimps are used to space beads on illusion or floating necklaces and they can even look quite decorative. Measure the strand for the necklace and decide where the bead or beads should go. Attach a crimp and add a bead or beads and another crimp. Hold the strand up so that the crimp drops down next to the beads, then secure with crimping pliers. Check each crimp individually to ensure that it won't slip before continuing. When adding a fastening to a piece of jewelry made with bead stringing wire, you can either use a crimp inside a calotte (bead tip), or using a crimp, loop the wire through the fastening and the crimp again and secure with crimping pliers. You can also use crimps to hold a beaded section in the center of a strand to prevent the clasp from sliding around to the front of the necklace. Thread the beads as usual and when centralized, fix into place with a crimp at each end. These crimps will not be obvious, but you can add crimp covers to hide them. These are fitted over the crimps with large crimp pliers and look like small, round metal beads (see Question 41).

*BELOW* Crimping is used here to create loops, and to hold beads in place on this illusion necklace.

# Question 79:
# When is bead stringing wire useful?

Bead stringing wire is one of the strongest materials for stringing beads and can be used for necklaces with heavy beads such as stone, large glass beads, or gemstones. Also, because of its resistance to wear, it is perfect for stringing metal beads and charms, or beads with sharp edges like bugles. Crystal beads have facets that can wear, so using bead stringing wire will prevent breakages and the loss of expensive beads.

You can buy beading wire in many colors and thicknesses, which allows you to either cover it completely with beads or space the beads, allowing the wire to become part of the design. Although some modern bead stringing wires can be knotted, you generally use crimps to secure or space beads. You can use bead stringing wire with a bead thread to create a knotted design when using heavy beads. Simply thread the beads one at a time onto both strands, tie the thread over the wire with an overhand knot, and then string the next bead. Continue until all the beads are added and then attach a fastening.

If you choose wire with the correct number of strands, it will drape beautifully no matter what weight of beads you use (see also Question 54).

*BELOW* Bead stringing wire in a coil.

# Question 80:
# What is gimp and how do I use it?

Gimp (sometimes called French wire or bullion) is a tiny, tightly packed spring that is most often used with silk thread in knotted pearl necklaces to prevent the thread from fraying as it rubs against the metal necklace fastening. It is available in gold and silver as well as bright metallic colors that you can color-coordinate with contemporary threads. You will also find gimp in different thicknesses – choose one with an inner diameter that will fit your thread closely in order to create a smooth and attractive loop. In a knotted necklace, string the last two beads without knots and then thread about 10–12 mm of gimp. String the

fastening and then take the thread back through the first bead so that the gimp forms a small loop through the fastening. Pull up to leave a small gap between the last two beads. Tie an overhand knot between these two beads, then take the thread through the next bead and trim. Gimp is not necessary with bead stringing wires but can be used with other bead stringing threads to prevent wear, and can be used whether the necklaces are finished with knots, calottes, bell cone ends, or crimps.

*BELOW* Gimp is used here to protect the thread as it passes through the loops of the finding.

# Question 81:
## How are cord necklaces created and finished?

Beading cords, such as waxed cotton and rat-tail, as well as round and flat cord, are a major part of the necklace design; they enhance the beads rather than get covered up by them. Choose the colors to complement the beads; a cord the same color as the beads but in a different tone such as a bright purple with a pastel purple cord will give a subtle effect. Using contrasting colors — orange cords with turquoise beads, or green with red — will create a more vibrant effect. You can also find variegated or space dyed silk cords, which are stunning when strung with beads.

You can string two cords through beads with large holes, or work with cord and thin waxed cotton together. This allows you to knot your cords in different ways and thread any beads with smaller holes on the waxed cotton only. The simplest way to use two colors of cord is to knot them both at once, creating a multicolored knot. Alternatively, you can knot one color over the other, and then knot them the other way, creating a pattern of alternating colored knots.

You can knot between beads, or space beads on the cord using individual knots, and even knot in small charms or wire coils (see Question 87). When your necklace reaches the required length, treat the ends to prevent fraying and hold in a specialized finding, such as a cord crimp, spring ends, cord ends, or even cord cones (see Question 36). Alternatively, the ends can simply be knotted on a longer necklace or a sliding fastening (see Question 86).

# Question 82:
# Do ribbon and metal mesh ribbons need different techniques?

Ribbon and metal mesh ribbons (also known as metallic mesh tubular ribbons or wire lace ribbons) add interest to jewelry designs. The ribbons can be used as a component of a necklace or bracelet or as a fastening. You can use ribbon to string a necklace if the holes are large enough, or you can string the beads on bead stringing wire and create a small loop at each end with crimps. Loop a double length of ribbon through each loop and tie the ribbon in a bow at the back of your neck. Short lengths of ribbon can be tied between the beads to add texture. Metal mesh ribbon is an extremely versatile material that can be manipulated in many ways. You can thread beads onto the mesh ribbon and either knot between beads or pull the mesh apart to create interesting shapes between the beads. Alternatively, push beads down the middle of the tube and knot to space the beads, or thread donut or washer-shaped beads onto the ribbon to space the enclosed beads. Crimp bar ends, which are available in a range of widths, can be used to secure the ends of ribbon, or if you have several strands, they can be secured inside a cone.

*FAR LEFT* This cord necklace uses knots to space the beads.

*LEFT* This necklace uses fabric and metal mesh ribbon to great effect.

**Stringing and Knotting**   97

# Question 83:
# How do I string beads onto memory wire?

Memory wire is very useful for creating jewelry that can be worn by anyone, regardless of size. It is a very hard wire that holds its circular shape, and can be cut to make a single ring or several coils. Memory wire is available in ring, bracelet, and necklace sizes. You can create a beautiful piece of jewelry very quickly, as you don't need a fastening. Simply attach a special end bead that has a hole on one side, or create a small loop in the wire with round-nose pliers.

Cut the wire to size with heavy-duty wire cutters (ordinary jewelry tools will get damaged), and file the ends to remove any sharp edges. Put a dot of beading or jewelry glue into the hole on the end bead and stick firmly to the end of the wire. Leave it to dry. Alternatively, make a loop on the end, then thread on your beads. You can completely fill the wire or use crimps to space the beads on the wire. Finish the necklace with either a loop or matching end bead. Vary your designs by incorporating jump rings, stringing chain between the beads or adding metal charms. If you want to create texture, add drop beads and gemstone chips.

*BELOW* Memory wire can have small balls glued to the ends to hold the beads on.

# Question 84:
# How do I design a multistrand necklace?

A multistrand necklace is a necklace with more than one strand. The multiple strands can start at the back of the neck or begin further down the necklace. There are five main types of multistrand necklaces, which are outlined in the table below.

| Type of Multistrand | Description |
| --- | --- |
| Parisian Loop | Classic design traditionally used with pearls. Two strands with a difference in length of 1–3 in. (2.5–8 cm). Both strings are attached to a clasp. |
| Increasing Loops | This is much bolder than the Parisian. It has several strands of beads, each made slightly longer, and all the strands are connected to a fastening. Each strand can have a different type of bead, or all the strands can have a mixture of matching beads. |
| Similar Loops | Making all of the strands roughly the same length gives a chunkier, fuller effect. This necklace works best with smaller beads, and the beads should get smaller toward the clasp. |
| Single to Multistrand | This necklace has a single strand at the back of the necklace that separates into two or more strands at the front. |
| Formal Multistrand | The formal style uses multistrand end bars and spacers to hold rows of beads at specific distances. Top rows should have fewer beads than the bottom rows to allow the necklace to drape neatly. |

Once you have decided on your overall design, you can choose the beads – remember that your beads will be tightly packed, so you need to think about using large and small beads to make the strands fit closely together. A beading board will help you lay out multiple strands of beads, and you may find an EZ necklace or jewelry bust useful for final bead adjustments, as they allow you to see how the strands will lie when worn.

Choose the string depending on how you want the necklace to hang; silk thread will drape softly, beading wire has a firmer drape, and braided thread can be used for small holed beads. Remember that not all of your strands need to be strung on the same material – for example, you may want to mix ribbons and cords, or metal ribbon and bead stringing wire. You may find it helpful to string your beads without completely finishing the ends with calottes or crimps so you can make adjustments. You can then choose the findings that will best suit your necklace.

# Question 85:
# What is a floating necklace?

A floating or illusion necklace has a fantastic delicacy. It is designed to showcase individual beads spaced along almost invisible bead thread with the beads seeming to "float" in the air.

A floating necklace is generally made with Illusion cord — a transparent nylon single strand thread — or you can use a bead stringing wire to hang the beads. For illusion necklaces, use a thicker thread for the main strand, with some beads added before lengths of finer thread are tied along the necklace to hang down. You can simply loop the thread through beads and tug to hold as the thread kinks, but a dot of instant (super) glue is more secure. Larger beads can be secured with a half hitch, too (see Question 89). If you push the bead up slightly after adding a dot of glue, the knot will be hidden inside the bead.

With bead stringing wire, the beads are held in place with crimps. Use tubular crimps, flattened with snipe-nose pliers, or crimp beads secured with crimp pliers for the neatest finish. You can also add crimp covers, which look like small metal beads once fitted over the crimps (see Question 40).

# Question 86:
# How do I create a sliding knot fastening?

The sliding knot fastening is the simplest and cheapest fastening, requiring no findings or tools. It is used to finish pendants and necklaces with only a few beads in the center of the necklace, or can be used to make a simple bracelet fastening.

- Thread the beads or pendant onto the cord, allowing about 6 in. (15 cm) at each end for the fastening.
- Lay it out on a flat surface in a circle so that ends overlap, leaving the two 6 in. (15 cm) tails.
- Tie the fastening with an overhand knot: pass the left-hand end over and back under the right-hand cord, then back over itself and through the loop to create a knot (see Question 87).
- Pull this tight around the right-hand cord. Repeat this on the right-hand side, so that two knots are created, facing away from each other.
- Pull the tail ends to fasten the necklace or bracelet, and pull the knots apart to open. The sliding knot fastening can also be used to adjust the length of a necklace.

*BELOW* Sliding knot fastenings are very useful for creating a pendant necklace with a waxed cord.

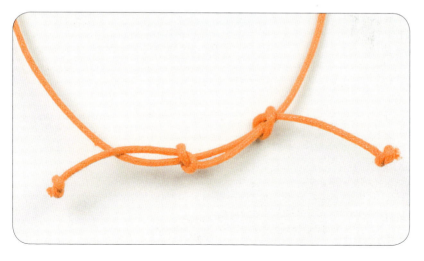

# Question 87:
# How do I make an overhand knot?

The overhand knot is one of the most useful knots in beading and the easiest knot to tie. It is used to tie bundles of threads together, to join new threads at the edge of bead loom work, or to knot between beads where there is only one thread.

The overhand knot is the shape of a pretzel.

- Cross the tail over the main thread to make a small loop.
- Pass it under the thread and back through the loop.
- You can move the position by putting an awl into the main loop of the knot and sliding it gently down toward the bead until it is in the correct position.
- Once the knot is tight around the needle, remove it and give it a final tug.

The double-overhand knot is a bulkier knot, ideal for beads with larger holes. This method uses more thread and is better than tying an overhand knot with much thicker thread. Tie it by making a loop and feeding the end twice through the main loop. This knot can also be moved and controlled with a blunt needle or awl. Allow extra thread when stringing a knotted necklace — 5 mm for each knot on ordinary thread and more with thicker thread.

# Question 88:
# How do I tie a reef (square) knot?

The reef or square knot is used to attach two threads together and is used as a decorative knot for macramé. It should be tied using two threads of equal thickness, and is used when you are knotting with two cords through the center of each bead. Allow approximately twice the length of the finished piece for each thread.

- Pass the left thread over the right and tuck it under.
- Pass the right thread over the left and out through the gap in the middle.
- If you get this knot in the wrong place, loosen it by pulling one end back over the knot, then re-tie.

# Question 89:
# What other knots are useful?

## Slipknot
A slipknot is very handy; it is used to create the first loop in both knitting and crochet and can be used as a quick stop knot because it is easily undone. The working thread (actually being used to knit or string) is the one able to pull through the knot to make the loop larger and smaller.

- Cross the tail behind the working thread and hold it between your index finger and thumb so that the loop faces toward you.
- Take the working thread behind the loop and pull it through.
- Pull the tail to tighten the knot and the working thread to adjust the size of the loop.

## Lark's head knot
- Make a loop in the working thread and pass it through a jump ring of the fastening.
- Feed the ends of the thread through the loop and pull tight.

### EXPERT TIP
❝ For a more secure fastening, use the surgeon's knot, a variation of the reef knot. Simply loop the thread under a second time when tying to make a knot that doesn't slip. ❞

## Figure eight
The figure eight knot is used in climbing to prevent ropes from slipping, because it does not unravel easily. Because these knots are large and do not come undone easily, they are perfect for using with calottes and clamshells.

- Cross the tail over the working thread and hold the loop between your index finger and thumb.
- Take the tail behind the main thread and go through the loop from the front.
- Pull both ends to tighten the knot, and add a drop of glue for extra security if you are going to cut the ends very short.

## Half-hitch knot
The half-hitch is used to secure thread ends when bead stitching or doing loom work.

- Take the needle behind a thread in the bead work to leave a loop.
- Pass the needle back through the loop and pull tight to make the first half hitch.
- Repeat for added security and thread the tail through several beads before trimming.

# Question 90:
# How do I tie a half-knot twist?

A half-knot twist is a macramé knot that creates a twisted cord. These knots are most often tied with a firm thread such as waxed cotton or hemp. You can add beads to the outer or core threads to create a beaded necklace.

- Secure four threads onto the work surface. Take the left thread under the core and over the right thread.
- Take the right thread over the core and through the loop formed by the left thread. Pull the knot tight.
- Repeat this knot in the same way, over and over until you have the full length.

It is important to always begin with the left thread in order to make the knots spiral neatly. If you tie the knots beginning with the right-hand thread, it will spiral in the opposite direction.

Once you have tied the knots, you can twist them around the core in order to make a tighter or looser coil.

**Adding beads**
To add beads, you can string beads on each outer thread between knots, or string a single bead in the two core threads so that it is wrapped by the outer cords and trapped between two knots. This technique can be used to create a multithread necklace, as you can tie the working threads around a core thread of any number of strands, which can then be beaded.

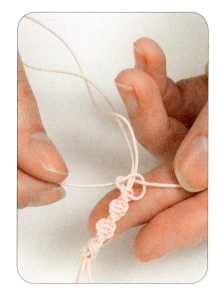

*RIGHT* A half-knot twist.

# Question 91:
# How do I tie a square-flat knot?

The square knot is a reef knot (see Question 88) generally worked over two core threads. It forms a flat band, which can be used to create an attractive choker or bracelet. You can make a wider band by starting with more cords and alternating the cords used for the knots.

For the basic band, the central core needs to be the length of the finished piece, plus 6 in. (15 cm) at each end for finishing. The working threads need to be at least three times longer.

• Fix the four threads firmly at one end, so that the working cords are on either side of the central core.
• Pass the right cord under the core and over the left cord.
• Take the left cord over the core and through the loop on the right. Pull the knot tight.
• Take the left cord under the core and over the right cord.
• Finish the knot by taking the right cord over the core and through the loop on the left. Repeat the entire knot.

Threading large beads onto the central core and tying one or two knots between each bead can enhance this band of flat knots. The working cords will frame the beads,

and if you choose a good contrast, you can create a really exciting effect.

You can also thread small beads onto the working cords between each knot; since these are only threaded onto one cord, you could even use seed beads (see Question 8).

*BELOW* A square-flat knot.

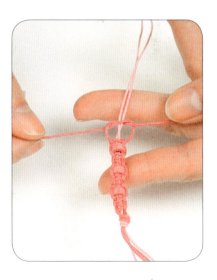

**92** How do I effectively work with thread?

**93** What is a workable length of thread?

**94** What is the best way of adding and finishing threads?

**95** How do I deal with thread ends?

**96** How do I correct my mistakes?

**97** My work is too tight — how do I fix it?

**98** My weave is very loose — how do I tighten it?

**99** What do "circle through," "pass through," and "pass back through" mean?

**100** How do I follow a chart?

**101** Can I use more than one bead stitch in the same piece?

**102** What is ladder stitch?

**103** How do I stitch two-drop ladder?

**104** What is brick stitch?

**105** What is the difference between in-and-out bead starts?

**106** How do I increase brick stitch?

**107** Do I have to start brick stitch with ladder stitch?

**108** How do I make a circular piece with a large central bead?

**109** What is herringbone stitch?

**110** Do I have to start with ladder stitch?

**111** How do I shape herringbone stitch?

**112** What is twisted herringbone?

**113** What is peyote stitch?

**114** What is the difference between odd- and even-count peyote?

**115** How do I shape peyote stitch?

**116** Why use square stitch and not a loom?

**117** How do I stitch square stitch?

**118** How do I shape square stitch?

**119** What is right-angle weave?

# 6
# BEAD WEAVING

Bead weaving is also called bead stitching or needle weaving. The beads are woven together using different stitches to create flat sections of fabric, tubes, or three-dimensional designs.

**120** How do I create a more open weave?

**121** How do I shape right-angle weave?

**122** What is chain stitch?

**123** What is freestyle bead weaving?

**124** What is horizontal netting?

**125** How do I shape horizontal netting?

**126** How do I create vertical netting?

**127** Can I work vertical netting in the round?

**128** What is a spiral rope?

**129** How do I make spiral rope?

**130** Is there a way of modifying spiral rope?

**131** What is the difference between ropes and tubes?

**132** How do I stitch in a tube?

**133** How do I work African helix?

**134** How do I make a daisy necklace?

**135** What is Nepal chain?

**136** What is St. Petersburg chain?

# Question 92:
# How do I effectively work with thread?

Threads can either have a round cross-section or a flat cross-section. Multifilaments such as Nymo, a type of waxed nylon thread, are flat and thread fairly easily through a beading needle as the eye is long and thin. Braided threads or cords are round, and you will find a fine sewing needle with a small round eye easier to thread. The best tool you can have for threading a needle is a pair of very sharp scissors; this will allow you to make clean cuts to the thread, preferably at an angle, which enables it to be easily passed through the eye of the needle. Bear in mind that because of the way needles are made, one side of the hole is slightly larger than the other. It is also easier to hold the thread between your thumb and index finger and bring the needle down onto it than to hold up the needle and bring the thread to it. Because thread comes on a tightly wound reel, it tends to reform the spiral and can easily tie itself into knots. To prevent this, simply hold a length of thread in your hands and pull tight, stretching it as firmly as you can. This should be enough to straighten the thread, but you can run it through thread conditioner as well to help prevent knots (see also Question 68).

*BELOW* When threading a needle, always take the needle to the thread.

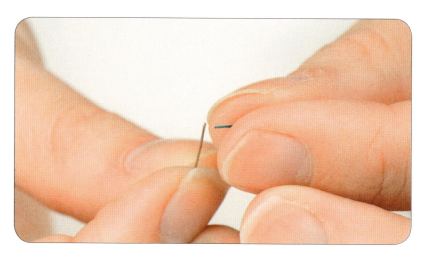

# Question 93:
# What is a workable length of thread?

The workable length will vary depending on the work you are doing and on your personal preference. Generally speaking, a thread the length of your outstretched arms is the longest you can comfortably work with for bead weaving. Each time you try a new technique, try different lengths of thread until you find the perfect length for you. Start with the longest length you think will be workable and then, if you find it is too long to work with, trim a piece off until you have the right length for you.

If your thread is very long, it is more likely to tangle but you can wax or condition the threads to prevent this from happening so much.

Braided threads such as Fireline are less likely to tangle than multi-filaments like Nymo or S-Lon. Longer threads do take more time to draw through the beads with each stitch you make, but with shorter lengths you will have to join in new threads more often. Shorter lengths of thread are worked less often through the beads, so they do not have as much chance to fray and wear. It can be beneficial to use shorter lengths when working on pieces that will have to bear weight as long as the ends are sewn in securely.

*BELOW* Different beading techniques require varying lengths of thread.

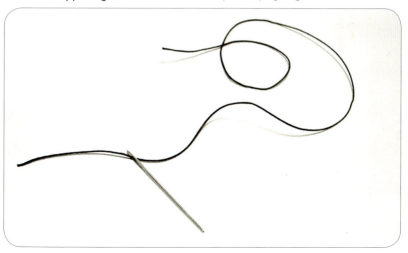

# Question 94:
# What is the best way of adding and finishing threads?

The key to sewing in threads quickly and neatly is to stop weaving before the thread gets too short. It is always tempting to finish just one more row, but you will find it much easier if you leave a 6 in. (15 cm) tail.

You need to ensure that your ends are carefully woven in so that they won't work their way out and allow your work to unravel. Weave the thread in back and forward, diagonally if possible, through the beads to keep it firmly in place. Working a half-hitch (see Question 89) once or twice will also anchor the thread securely.

It is better to begin and finish threads in the middle of your work rather than at the edge. Leave the old thread end hanging out so that you can see where you finished until you weave in the new thread, then you will see where to bring the thread out to continue. By the time you have woven in several ends, particularly on a complex piece, you may need to use a finer needle to get the threads through the beads. If you find you cannot weave in your old end, work another section with the new thread; these beads will have plenty of space to weave in the old thread.

*BELOW* Tying a half-hitch knot.

# Question 95:
# How do I deal with thread ends?

After you've woven the ends of your threads to secure them, there will still be tails emerging from the beads. It is always better to have the thread coming out from the beadwork rather than at the edge, and then to leave them until you've finished your work and can deal with them all at once using one of these three methods:

• Use really sharp scissors to trim the tail as close to the work as possible, preferably on the reverse side. When finishing bead loomwork, remember that the warp thread runs down the side and you must be extra careful not to cut through it. Minimize the risk by bringing the needle out between the beads in the middle of the work. By trimming the end between two beads, you will be able to get much closer to the work without cutting important threads.

• You can also burn away thread ends using a thread burner, which heats up at the end and burns or melts the threads. Be careful not to heat too much, or you may sever other threads by accident.

• Alternatively, insert the needle inside the row next to the thread end and put the thread through the eye of the needle; trim it short and then draw the needle through the row. The end will be drawn into the work and left inside. A big-eye needle is ideal for this technique.

*BELOW* Using a thread burner to remove loose ends.

# Question 96:
# How do I correct my mistakes?

There are lots of different bead stitches, but when mistakes occur the problem is usually the wrong bead or too many beads in the work; the solution for each stitch is often quite similar. When you have made a mistake it is very tempting to immediately put your needle back through the beads; this is almost guaranteed to make it worse, as you may catch fibers on other threads. Instead, take the needle off the thread and carefully draw the thread back through – a blunt needle will help with this – until you have undone the mistake, then re-thread the needle and continue more carefully. If you are only going back through one bead, you can reverse the needle and go back through eye first if the tail of the thread is long enough.

A more frustrating problem is getting the needle stuck inside a bead. Rather than risk breaking the bead, push the needle back through by holding it with flat-nose pliers for safety and then change to a smaller size needle. You may find that putting the tip of the needle onto a cutting mat will allow you to ease the needle until it becomes loose. Mark the spot with a small sticker so that you don't try to weave in an end through the same place.

## EXPERT TIP

❝ If you have woven or stitched the wrong bead or an extra bead into your work, you can crush it with flat-nose pliers. Insert a needle or pin into the bead and then crush it with pliers; the needle will prevent the thread from snapping. ❞

# Question 97:
# My work is too tight — how do I fix it?

When your work is too tight, the beadwork becomes distorted and doesn't lie the way you expect; if you work jewelry too tightly with bead weaving, it will not drape well around the neck or wrist. Some pieces such as tubes or vessels do need to be worked at quite a high tension so that they stand up well, but if you make it too tight the sides start to collapse. In general, you should avoid tugging the thread too tightly as you work, but a simple technique to reduce tension is to relax and put your work down frequently — this allows the thread to loosen slightly each time you stop and prevents the beading from becoming too tight. You could also use round beads rather than cylinder beads, as they don't fit together so neatly. Gloss beads slide against one another more because of the slippery coating, which means they do not sit as tightly together and the finished piece is more flexible.

If the thread fills the hole in the beads, it is less likely to ease out as you stitch, so working with beads with a larger hole and thinner thread will help keep the tension loose.

*BELOW* With circular bead stitching, it is important to keep a loose tension so that the bead motif lies flat. Tight stitching will create a bowl shape.

# Question 98:
# My weave is very loose – how do I tighten it?

If you work loosely, your beading can be too floppy to hold its shape. Loose bead weaving is also a problem, as thread ends easily work their way out and the beaded piece can fall to bits. Adding a stop bead or bead stopper spring at the beginning of your work will help keep the tension up, as you can tighten the work against it in the first few rows. You can also secure the thread with a half-hitch knot (see Question 89) from time to time to prevent the threads from loosening.

Coating the threads with conditioner or beading wax makes the thread slightly sticky and prevents it from slipping back through the beads as you work (see Question 68). If you don't like using conditioner, try doubling your threads; this will fill the holes in the beads and stiffen your work. You may find it more difficult to sew in your ends, but you can leave a long tail and sew in each thread separately with a fine needle.

Using smaller beads with the same-sized thread will produce tighter work – remember that it is hole size that is important here, not bead diameter, so a piece worked with Japanese cylinder beads and a piece worked in seed beads with the same outer diameter will have different tensions.

*BELOW* Use a bead stopper to maintain tension in your work.

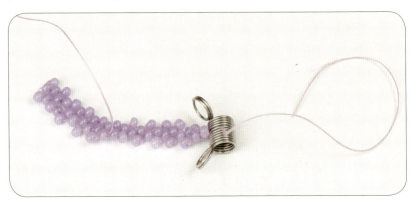

# Question 99:
# What do "circle through," "pass through," and "pass back through" mean?

These terms all have to do with the way you take the thread through a bead in bead weaving. If you take the needle the wrong way through a bead, your needle is likely to end up in the wrong place, or beads may not be held securely in your work.

## Circle through

To circle through a bead, you go through it again, in the same direction as you went through it originally. If you worked this with only one bead, it would create a loop of thread around the outside of the bead. If you work it through two beads, they are joined by the loop of thread.

## Pass back through

This is where you take the thread through the bead in the opposite direction from the last time you took the needle through it. If you tried to do this with one bead, the thread would simply form a loop and be drawn back out of the bead.

## Pass through

This is the simplest direction to understand. All you have to do is take the needle through the bead in the direction you are currently working. You do not need to worry about which direction the last thread was going in. This could be used for picking up a new bead, or to instruct you to go through an existing bead or even a whole row.

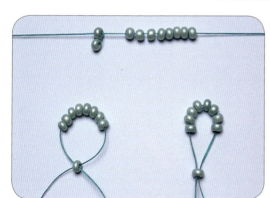

*LEFT* Make sure you take the thread through the bead in the correct direction

*Top beads:* Circle through

*Left beads:* Pass back through

*Right beads:* Pass through

# Question 100:
# How do I follow a chart?

Beading charts for each of the bead stitches are quite different because of the way the beads are positioned on the finished piece. A square-stitch chart is usually a basic square grid, so you can use cross-stitch charts to create a pattern in beadwork. It is not absolutely accurate since seed beads are not square; they are slightly wider than they are tall. You can find charts that look like individual beads, and these are more accurate. Peyote (see Question 113) and brick stitch (see Question 104) charts are similar. The brick stitch chart looks like a brick wall, and if you rotate the chart 90 degrees you will have a peyote chart. Herringbone (see Question 109) charts have the beads lying at an angle so that they form columns of "v" shapes that correspond to the columns. Right-angle weave charts have the beads in a square formation. You work in blocks of four beads either up and down or backward and forward across the chart. It is important to begin the design at the right point in the chart, especially when working in peyote stitch. If you are unsure, work a test piece to check the order that you pick up the beads and where to begin. To avoid losing your place, highlight the rows as you go along, or use a ruler or a Post-it note on the pattern to mark your place. If you are going to use the same pattern again, cover it with acetate and dot each bead with a marker.

*LEFT* If you rotate this Peyote stitch chart 90 degrees, it can be used to create brick stitch patterns.

# Question 101:
# Can I use more than one bead stitch in the same piece?

Bead weaving is often worked in the same stitch, as people have favorite stitches that they like to use. Working two or more stitches on the same piece can add interest to a design.

- Peyote (see Question 113) and herringbone (see Question 109) stitches form beautiful ruffles that you can use to add a decorative edging to pieces worked in square stitch (see Question 116), ladder stitch (see Question 102), and brick stitch (see Question 104). The new stitches have a different texture and add interest to your work.
- Peyote stitch also has beautiful feathered edges, which you can emphasize with drop beads for an attractive finish.
- Generally, flat pieces are worked in one stitch but when you begin to increase or shape the work, it can be beneficial to introduce another stitch. It is easier to swap between some stitches than others – sometimes you can add beads onto the outer threads, or you can change stitches within the beading.
- When working a bezel around a cabochon, for example, you can begin with a peyote stitch and then introduce two beads instead of one in the next round to create a base row for herringbone stitch.
- Peyote stitch is often worked between columns of herringbone stitch to increase and create exquisite shapes. To increase in herringbone stitch, you generally add floating beads; to use peyote stitch instead, simply weave the needle through beads in the previous row rather than allowing them to float. The peyote stitch makes the resulting beading much firmer and allows you to create unusual three-dimensional shapes.

*BELOW* Using more than one stitch allows you to make exciting 3-D pieces.

# Question 102:
# What is ladder stitch?

Ladder stitch is generally a single row of beads stitched together to form a flat band, but the ends can be joined to create a tube. Ladder stitch can be easily stitched and then embellished with bugle beads or with a mixture of seed and bugle beads. Younger children can make bangles with cord and large beads, or make a simple ring or bangle for a friend by stitching with thin elastic instead of thread.

Ladder stitch can be used as the base for both brick and herringbone stitches. Brick stitch is worked into the threads running along the edges of the ladder stitch band, and herringbone stitch is worked through the bugles. Ladder stitch is most easily learned using bugles because they are easy to hold as you

stitch. There are several techniques for creating ladder stitch, but this technique is perfect for beginners.
- Pick up two bugles and circle through both again, then pull up so that they are sitting side by side.
- Pick up another bugle and circle through the previous bead and the bead just added.
- Continue adding beads until your work is the right length.
- If you want to create a tube, go through the first bugle and the last one again.
- Secure the thread tails using half-hitches and sewing them in (see also Questions 89 and 94).

*BELOW*
*Top box* Ladder stitch.
*Bottom box* Drop ladder stitch.

# Question 103:
# How do I stitch two-drop ladder?

Two-drop ladder stitch is generally worked with beads rather than bugles and is often used as a base for herringbone stitch, as there is not the strong contrast in appearance that you get with a bugle-ladder stitch band. Work the first row of herringbone stitch through the top row of beads only.

The key to stitching two-drop ladder is to think of each bead of ordinary ladder stitch as a rung. A rung could be one or more beads, but you always deal with it in the same way. In two-drop ladder, you use two beads on every rung, but you stitch through them as if they were a single bead. Three- and four-drop ladder stitch can be worked, too, but any wider than this and you will find that the rungs start to spread apart and flex too much.

## HOW IT'S DONE

**1** To stitch the basic two-drop ladder stitch, pick up four seed beads and circle through all the beads again.

**2** Pull both ends of the thread gently to bring the four beads tightly together.

**3** Pick up two beads and pass through the previous two beads (the second rung) and the two just added again.

**4** Pick up the next two beads. Circle back through the previous two beads, then pass through the two new beads.

**5** Continue adding new beads until the chain is the right length. You can two-drop with two beads on each rung, or alternate one rung with two beads and one with a single short bugle.

## EXPERT TIP

**❝ You can create a different texture and a wider piece of work by using the two-drop method. Pick up four beads instead of two, and then go through the first loop of the row below, then back through the last two beads before picking up the next two beads. Continue in the same way, adding two beads instead of one at each step. ❞**

# Question 104:
# What is brick stitch?

Brick stitch is an attractive flat stitch that is fairly stiff, as the beads butt together like a brick wall. It will bend along its width but not along the length of the piece. Bear this in mind when you are designing your work, as you can make tubular vessels easily. However, the stitch is not suitable for making bags or amulet purses with a flap that folds over the top.

Brick stitch is different from the other bead stitches because it is worked by passing the needle through the threads that hold the beads together rather than through the previous beads. It is most easily worked from a base of ladder stitch (see Question 102); if the ladder stitch is worked with bugles, and the brick stitch with seed beads, the ladder stitch will form an attractive border.

- Begin with the thread coming out of the top of the first bead in the ladder stitch row (flip the ladder stitch row over if the thread is coming from the bottom of the bead).
- Pick up two beads. Pass the needle under the loop of thread between the first two beads of the ladder stitch.
- Take the needle back through the second bead and pull the thread taut.
- Pick up another bead and take the needle under the next loop of thread.
- Go back through the bead just added and pull the thread taut.
- Continue to the end of the row, adding one bead at a time.
- To begin the next and subsequent rows, always pick up two beads to start and then add one at a time.

*BELOW* Brick stitch.

# Question 105:
# What is the difference between in- and out- bead starts?

Brick stitch has the appearance of a brick wall, with each bead overlapping by half the two beads below. When building a brick wall, you add half bricks at the ends to create a straight face; you can't add half a bead, however, so there is always a pattern of inset and overhanging beads. You can vary these to alter the shaping of the piece, or alternate in- and out-bead rows to create as smooth and even a side as possible.

**In-bead start**
This is where you begin a row with the first bead in the row set in one space.
**In-bead end**
The last bead in the row is set back so that there is a half bead after it.
**Out-bead end**
The last bead of the row will extend out beyond the last bead.
**Out-bead start**
A row beginning with the first bead overhanging by half a bead.

# Question 106:
# How do I increase brick stitch?

Increasing and decreasing brick stitch is easier than with most stitches because you use the brick pattern of the stitch to work the decrease and increase.

To increase the piece, work an out-bead end, and then an out-bead start on the next row. Finish the row with another out-bead end and begin the next row with another out-bead. Continue adding rows, always ending and beginning with out-beads until the work is the width you require.

To decrease your work, finish on an in-bead end, and then begin with an in-bead start. At the other end, you can repeat the decrease with an in-bead end and another in-bead start.

*BELOW* Increasing your brick stitch is relatively simple to do.

# Question 107:
## Do I have to start brick stitch with ladder stitch?

If you don't want the contrast between the ladder stitch border and brick stitch, you can work a double-row base instead. This technique looks like two rows of brick stitch, and you will not notice any join as you continue in brick stitch if you use the same beads for the start and the brick stitch. The double-row base is also the ideal way to begin brick stitch when you are using unusual beads that have a larger diameter than bugles. If you use cubed beads, for example, the brick effect will be enhanced, and because the beads butt closely together, the fabric will be almost inflexible.

*BELOW* Brick stitch on a row of ladder stitch.

# Question 108:
# How do I make a circular piece with a large central bead?

You can create circular pieces with almost any beading stitch, but brick stitch creates a particularly beautiful flat circle with a solid center, which is ideal for the base of a round container, or to create a rosette.

## EXPERT TIP

❝ The double-row base is also the ideal way to begin brick stitch when you are using unusual beads that have a larger diameter than bugles. If you use cubed beads, for example, the brick effect will be enhanced, and because the beads butt closely together, the fabric will be almost inflexible. ❞

## HOW IT'S DONE

**1** Begin with a large bead, 6 in. (15 cm) from the end of the thread. Take the needle back through the bead four times so that there are two loops of thread down opposite sides of the large bead.

**2** Pick up two beads and pass the needle under the thread loops on one side.

**3** Take the needle back through the second bead added and then pick up another bead, taking the thread through the loop of thread again, and then back through the bead just added.

**4** Continue working brick stitch around the bead until you return to the first bead. Loop the thread through the first and last beads to hold them firmly together, and ensure that the thread is on the outside.

You must begin each new row with the double-bead start, and work the row around adding single beads each time. Increase the number of beads on this row by using one or two of the loops twice. You can lay the beads out around the center to work out how many increases you will need on each row, and where you will place them.

# Question 109:
# What is herringbone stitch?

Herringbone or Ndebele stitch is a distinctive stitch where the beads are added in pairs to form tiny v-shapes. It is a more complex stitch to learn, but its attractive chevron pattern makes it worth persevering. Because the beads are added two at a time, it is a quick stitch to work. Beginners will find it easier to begin herringbone on a base row of two-drop ladder stitch.

## HOW IT'S DONE

**1** Hold the ladder stitch base so that the working thread comes out of the top of the last bead of the base. Pick up two beads and take the needle down through the next two beads of the ladder stitch and up through the next two beads.

**2** Pick up two beads and take the needle down through the next two beads on the ladder stitch and so on.

**3** When you reach the end of the ladder stitch, pick up the last two beads and take the needle down through the last bead of the base.

**4** Go across and up through the second bead in, and then go back across again to emerge through the last bead added.

**5** On the first row of herringbone, pick up two beads and take the needle down through the end bead of the previous row.

**6** Pass the needle under the loop between the beads in the row below. Take the needle back up through the two end beads to begin the next row.

For tubular herringbone, you always step up at the end of a round through the two beads, one above the other, ready to begin the next round.

*LEFT* Herringbone worked on two-drop ladder stitch.

# Question 110:
# Do I have to start with ladder stitch?

It is not necessary to begin herringbone with a row of ladder stitch; you can create a special start, which creates a beautiful v-shaped edging on both edges. To make it easier for you to understand how the triple row start is formed, the example given will have three different colored vertical rows. Use a stop bead or spring to prevent the beads from slipping off the thread, and leave a long tail for sewing in.

*BELOW*  An example of herringbone with a triple row start.

# Question 111:
# How do I shape herringbone stitch?

It is preferable to shape herringbone stitch in the body of the work, as you get a big step when increasing or decreasing at the end of a row. The paired stitches mean that, when you add beads at the side, you have to add two, which creates the step effect. To decrease, simply stop beading before the last pair or "stack" of beads and work back along the row as normal. To increase, add a pair of beads using ladder stitch, and then work back along the row using herringbone stitch.

To maintain the smooth sides, you can increase and decrease between the stacks. If you are going to decrease between the stacks, you stitch every stack until you reach the point where you are going to

decrease. Instead of picking up two beads, take the thread across the gap and through the next bead as normal before picking up the next two beads. Tighten the thread to close the gap and then continue as normal. To decrease more gently, pick up a floating bead in the first row and no beads in the second.

To increase, add a single bead between two stacks and continue to the end of the row. When you reach that point again, pick up two beads and attach them to the new single bead. From there, you can stitch herringbone as usual or work herringbone stitch in the two floating beads, and then add a bead between each herringbone stitch in the next round and so on.

# Question 112:
# What is twisted herringbone?

Twisted herringbone is an attractive variant of tubular herringbone, where the beads slowly spiral around the outside of the tube. It is easier to learn by using different colors for each stack, as in this example (see also Question 132).

# Question 113:
# What is peyote stitch?

Peyote stitch comes from the Native Americans, who use this stitch to decorate costumes and objects used in peyote ceremonies, and is popular around the world. Once you get started, the stitch is reasonably easy to work, but beginners may find starting off confusing. Peyote stitch looks like brick stitch placed on its side and thus is more flexible horizontally, which makes it an ideal stitch for bags with flaps. Because the in- and out-beads at the top and bottom create a "zipper" effect, peyote can be easily formed into a tube. The method here is even-count peyote stitch (see Question 114 for odd-count peyote stitch).

*BELOW* In peyote stitch, the beads are worked lying on their sides.

## HOW IT'S DONE

**1** Pick up an even number of beads; these will form your first two rows. Because the rows overlap, if you pick up sixteen beads, the piece will be sixteen wide – each row will have eight beads on it.

**2** Pick up another bead, skip the bead next to it, and pass back through the next.

**3** Pick up another bead, skip one bead, and pass through the next. Continue in the same way until the end of the row; you should now have a series of connected h-shapes, with one bead sticking out in the middle on the end of the row.

**4** Take the needle through the bead sticking out, ready for the next row.

**5** Pick up another bead and pass through the last bead added on the previous row. From now on, simply pass through the beads that are sticking up, putting new beads in all the gaps until the piece is the correct length.

# Question 114:
# What is the difference between odd- and even-count peyote?

Odd- and even-count peyote stitches both look the same once the bead fabric is created, and the technique is the same except that you need to use a different method for turning at the end of the row. Odd-count peyote has an odd number of beads in each row, making it ideal for pictorial work or patterns. Because many designs are based on an odd number of beads, you can place the design centrally.

## EXPERT TIP

66 For a first attempt, use alternate color beads for the first two rows and then add another color so that the rows are more obvious. 99

## HOW IT'S DONE

**1** Pick up an odd number of beads and then work in the same way as even-count.

**2** Pick up another bead, skip the last bead, and pass back through the next bead.

**3** Continue picking up beads, skipping a bead and passing through the next to the end of the row.

**4** Tie the tail and main thread together at the end.

**5** Turn the work and pass through the last bead added.

**6** Work along the row, adding a bead between every "up" bead.

**7** When you get back to the end with the knotted tail, pass the needle through the thread at the edge before passing back through the last bead added to begin the next row. This little stitch, every second row, is a quick way to lock the end bead in position. Alternatively, you can weave through beads to come out at the correct point, ready to begin the next row.

# Question 115:
# How do I shape peyote stitch?

To shape peyote stitch, you have two choices – do you want a flat piece, or a wavy, frill effect? If you want to form a frill, you can increase or decrease by more than one bead in the same row, and keep that up for a few rows. The extra beads will force the bead fabric to buckle. For a flat effect when shaping, you need to keep the increase or decrease very gradual.

To increase within your work, bead along the row until you get to the point you want to increase. Instead of picking up one bead, pick up two and ease them into the gap. If the tension in your work is too tight this will not work. The two beads will sit in a slight v-shape. Finish the row, turn, and come back. When you reach the two new beads, add a bead before them as usual, and then add a bead between them and a bead after them. Continue to the end of the row. The next row can be beaded as normal.

To work a decrease, bead to the point you want to decrease and then pass the needle through two beads sticking up without adding a bead between them. Close the gap as much as possible by pulling the thread taut; the gap will be closed fully in the next few rows. On the next row, only put one bead above the decreased space, and the row after that will be worked normally.

## EXPERT TIP

66 It is a good idea to loosen the tension for the row prior to any increase so that the extra beads fit in. 99

# Question 116:
# Why use square stitch and not a loom?

Square stitch and loom work are almost indistinguishable, and you can work from the same chart for both techniques. (See Chapter 7 for more information on Bead Looming.) There are no particular aesthetic reasons for choosing one or the other, although square stitch is more flexible along its length and can be shaped by decreasing or increasing much more readily than loom work. Because a loom takes a while to set up, you will find it is far quicker to work small pieces in square stitch. For very large pieces the loom is almost indispensable – it is far easier to work big pieces when they are supported, and you will be able to see the pattern more clearly.

Another bonus of square stitch is that there are fewer ends to be sewn in, which makes it much more suitable for smaller pieces of shaped jewelry. Because each bead has threads passing through it several times, you will need to use beads with fairly large holes such as cylinder beads and a fine size 13 needle. If you want to use beads with very small holes, you can use a loom and the pulled-warp method (see Question 148), as this has the fewest possible threads passed through each bead.

*LEFT* A bracelet made using square stitch.

# Question 117:
# How do I stitch square stitch?

Square stitch is an easy stitch to learn, and it's easy to create patterns or designs because the beads are added in straight rows.

*BELOW* Square stitch produces a smooth, even fabric.

## HOW IT'S DONE

**1** Attach a stop bead or bead-stopper spring to the end of a long length of thread.

**2** Pick up the beads that will form the first row, and drop down to the stop-bead spring.

**3** Pick up a bead to begin the second row. Circle through the last bead of the first row and the bead just added to secure it.

**4** Pick up another bead, circle through the next bead along on the first row, and then pass through the new bead again. The new beads are suspended below the first row.

**5** Pick up the beads one at a time, circling through the bead above to secure each time. This technique will attach all the beads.

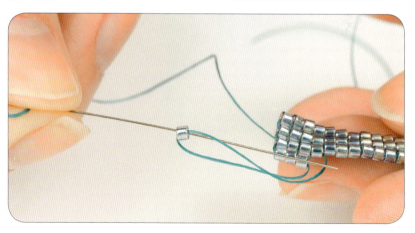

# Question 118:
## How do I shape square stitch?

You can increase or decrease on the outer edge for a stepped effect, or increase within the rows for a much smoother effect.

To decrease on one edge, when you weave back through the new row to stabilize it, come out before the last bead and add your first bead to the second bead on the previous row. Continue as usual to the end of the row, but when you weave through remember to bring your needle out one bead early to avoid an unsightly loop.

To increase by one bead on the edge, pick up two new beads. Circle back through the first bead, then through the second, and continue beading along the new row.

To work an increase within the row, pick up two beads instead of one at the point where you want to increase. Work the square stitch through a single bead on the row below, and then on the next row bead every stitch as usual.

*BELOW* An attractive beaded ring made using square stitch.

# Question 119:
# What is right-angle weave?

Right-angle weave (RAW) is a grid-like fabric made up of beads in a square formation so that each bead is at right angles to the next one. The stitch moves and drapes like fabric and can be used to cover bags, as well as to create beautiful pieces of jewelry.

Right-angle weave is quite complex because there are different numbers of beads to pick up each time, and the thread path is not always the same. It is easier to learn the stitch if you think always of making a box with each stitch; you have to make a base, two sides, and a lid for each box.

*BELOW* Right-angle weave.

## HOW IT'S DONE

**1** Pick up four beads on a long length of thread and tie in a circle. Pass through the beads again until the thread emerges at the top opposite the tail. This is the first box.

**2** Pick up three beads, and circle back through the bead you exited to make the next box. Your working thread is now between two boxes.

**3** Thread through the side and top of the new box, and pick up three more beads. Continue in the same way, adding three beads each time until your work is the right length.

**4** Circle through the beads again until your thread is exiting from a side bead of your last box.

**5** Pick up three beads, and circle back through the bead you exited to create the first box of the second row.

**6** Circle through the beads to get into the right position to add the next box. There are already two sides for this box, so you only need to pick up two beads. Continue in the same way until your work is complete.

# Question 120:
# How do I create a more open weave?

The size of your bead will determine the size of the hole in the middle of each unit, so four seed beads will have a closer appearance than four larger beads. However, you can increase the number of beads in each unit to create a more open weave. With right-angle weave, you can add extra beads between the four base beads. You can keep the units square by adding one or more beads between each of the four base beads, or you can add more beads lengthways to make elongated units, which are, for example, 1 bead wide and 6 beads long. Once you have mastered adding more beads to each side, you will be able to create some really stunning effects – adding bugle beads or crystals to the mix.

## HOW IT'S DONE

**1** In this example 3 x 3-drop, there are twelve beads in each box, three on each side. Pick up the first twelve beads, and circle through the first three beads to form a circle.

**2** Circle through the next six beads and add nine beads, circling back through the three beads you have just exited to create another loop on the weave.

**3** Continue until you have enough loops for the length of your work.

**4** Move the needle so that it exits the bottom of the last box.

**5** Add nine beads and move the needle so that you are in the right place to add the next two sides, and pick up only six beads.

**6** Continue adding these loops of beads until the piece is the right size.

## EXPERT TIP

66 **The same-sized weave, but with a far more regular shape, can be created by replacing the three seed beads with large bugles.** 99

# Question 121:
# How do I shape right-angle weave?

It is easier by far to shape right-angle weave on the edge of your work. You can do this very simply by adding an extra box to the side, or by missing a box entirely. Decreasing and increasing within the work is more complex. If you are using single beads on each side of the individual boxes, you will need to remove or add a whole box. If you are using a two-drop or more method, you can reduce the number of beads on the sides of each box – four on each side in the first row, three on each side in the second, for example.

If you want to decrease by removing a box, work as normal until you reach the point where you want to decrease, and then attach the beads for the next box through both the base of the box above and the base of the box next to it. Draw taut and reposition your needle, then continue the row. When you return along the row, simply bead on the existing boxes, skipping the space.

*BELOW* Another example of right-angle weave from Africa.

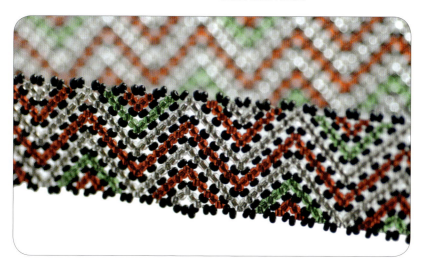

# Question 122:
# What is chain stitch?

Chain stitch is a variant of right-angle weave, which can be used to create long chains of bead work to form a necklace or bangle. You can vary the numbers of beads used on each side of the "box," add embellishments, use different types of beads, and use different threading materials to create different effects.

You will be using a figure-eight stitch to create each unit, which must have at least four beads in it. In this example, there are twelve beads in each unit.

## HOW IT'S DONE

**1** Pick up twelve seed beads on a long length of thread with a needle on each end.

**2** Place the beads in the middle of the string, and take one of the needles through three beads to create a circle. Pick up six beads on one needle and three on the other.

**3** Pass the needle with three beads through at least three beads on the other side to create a second unit. Continue alternating which needle picks up the six beads.

## EXPERT TIP

**“** Try working the chain with a long piece of monofilament. Put six beads on each side of the chain, and use a single bead to cross over the threads. This will form a beautiful rounded chain. **”**

*BELOW* Add texture to your chain stitch by adding drop beads.

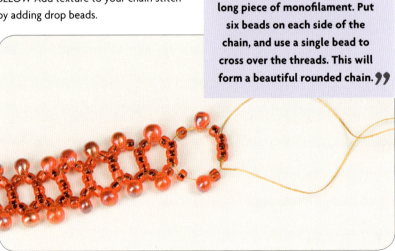

# Question 123:
# What is freestyle bead weaving?

Freestyle bead weaving, based on right-angle weave and chain stitch in this example, is used to make beautiful motifs that can be incorporated into pieces of jewelry. Bicone crystals and seed beads are particularly suitable for creating motifs like flowers, snowflakes, and butterflies. These can be worked and then incorporated into bead chains or attached to bead-weaving fabric.

Because the beads are at different angles, you usually follow a diagram instead of using a chart. Most diagrams show the shapes of beads used and show the direction the thread is going using arrows. The first and last beads are usually marked

with symbols such as asterisks. You simply begin at the asterisk and pick up the beads in each loop, taking the needle and thread through the beads exactly as shown. You can also draw out your own diagram or trace a motif. If you are not sure how to sew the beads together, try tracing over the entire design without lifting the pencil from the paper. It is important to work with a fairly stiff tension so that the motifs keep their shape. Experiment with different threads to see which gives the desired effect.

When stitching with crystals, you should use either a thread that is braided or monofilament, as these are more resistant to fraying.

# Question 124:
# What is horizontal netting?

Horizontal netting is worked with a single thread from side to side. It is often used to add an attractive border to fabric, and can be used to make collar-style necklaces or to cover beads. Each loop in the net has an even number of bridge beads and a central bead that will be shared by the loops in the next row. Three-bead and five-bead netting are the

most common styles, making a fairly compact netting fabric, but you can work much larger loops to create a loose netting on the edge of a scarf. You can either space loops of beads along the edge of fabric or begin with a string of beads.

# Question 125:
## How do I shape horizontal netting?

Horizontal netting is shaped by increasing and decreasing the number of bridge beads on each row. By adding more bridge beads, you will make the netting wider, and by using fewer bridge beads, you will make it narrower. Remember, you should increase or decrease the loops evenly by adding or taking away one bridge bead on either side of the shared bead, unless you want to work a freestyle piece of netting.

Horizontal netting can be shaped to create flat, circular pieces such as coasters or rosette embellishments, or you can shape the netting to cover three-dimensional objects such as beads and baubles. There is no set pattern for increasing and decreasing, as it depends on the shape and size of the beads. Experiment by working two or three rows the same for each increase, then if you are covering a bead or bauble try the beading out frequently to make sure the netting is following the shape neatly. You can always take back a row or two and adjust the bead quantities to get a better fit. Once you reach the center point, you need to keep the netting on the bead or bauble and decrease the beads in the same quantities you used for increasing. Finish the netting to match the other end.

*BELOW* Horizontal netting can be easily worked over beads.

# Question 126:
# How do I create vertical netting?

Vertical netting is worked with pairs of threads, which can be suspended from a multiring end bar, ribbon, a piece of fabric, or a string of beads. Vertical netting is suitable for a variety of end uses but is particularly suited where you want a fringe, tassels, or drop beads at the bottom of the netting. You can use vertical netting to make a pretty set of earrings by attaching pairs of thread to a multiring end bar. You do not need a needle on every thread, as you work each thread in turn, but a short big-eye needle (see Question 75) lets you swap from thread to thread quickly.

## EXPERT TIP

66 **Add vertical netted fringing to soft furnishings or scarves for a touch of luxury. Sew the fringing directly to the fabric, or stitch onto ribbon.** 99

## HOW IT'S DONE

**1** Attach a double thread to each ring using a lark's-head knot.

**2** Pick up a shared bead on each pair of threads.

**3** Separate the threads and pick up three bridge beads on each thread except the outer threads.

**4** Skipping the outer threads, pick up a shared bead on the remaining pairs of threads.

**5** Separate the threads again and pick up the next set of bridge beads, then the shared beads. You will find you need to add one or two extra bridge beads down the end threads so that the shared beads are in line.

**6** Continue until the netting is the length required, then add drop beads or create a fringe.

# Question 127:
## Can I work vertical netting in the round?

Vertical netting is easy to work in the round (also known as circular netting), and it lends itself to creating a tassel or fringing at the bottom of a large bead or bauble because of the multiple threads. If you are working over a round shape rather than in a straight line, you may find that having needles on two threads at a time will be helpful. Cut threads twice the length required and attach with a lark's-head knot.

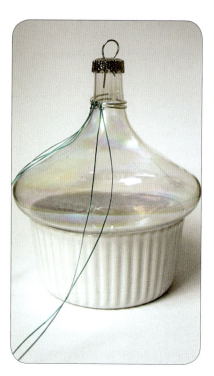

### HOW IT'S DONE

**1** To cover a bauble with netting, attach the working threads to a ring of wire around the top of the bauble.

**2** With the first thread, pick up a shared bead, a bridge bead, and a shared bead.

**3** With the second thread, pick up a shared bead and a bridge bead, then pass through the shared bead on the first thread.

**4** Move to the next pair of threads and repeat. On the next row, you have threads hanging in pairs from the shared beads; take one thread from each pair and pick up two bridge beads, a shared bead, three bridge beads, and a shared bead.

**5** Take the unbeaded thread of one pair and pick up two bridge beads.

**6** Go through the shared bead of the adjacent pair, pick up three bridge beads, and pass through the final shared bead of the pair thread.

**7** Continue all the way around the bauble. Keep adding rows until the bauble is half coved in beads, then add fringing to the bottom of the net.

*LEFT* Balance baubles on a small dish so that you can attach the threads easily and work the vertical netting.

# Question 128:
## What is a spiral rope?

A spiral rope is worked with a simple but versatile stitch, which is extremely strong because you stitch through the beads over and over again. It can be used as a necklace or bangle, or even as a bag strap for an attractive evening bag. Any beads can be used to create a spiral rope, but they are most often created with seed and bugle beads.

Two sets of beads are used – the core beads lie at the center of the rope and are threaded through at least three times, so you must make sure the holes are big enough. The outer beads form small loops that spiral around the core beads. You could use a few seed beads for each loop, or a combination of seed and drop beads, or even replace the smaller beads with a single long bugle for a dramatic effect. Spiral ropes use quite a lot of beads; if you are not sure if you have enough, work 2 in. (5 cm) of spiral and count how many beads you have used, and then work out the number you will need for the finished length.

*BELOW* These bracelets are both made from spiral rope.

# Question 129:
# How do I make spiral rope?

Spiral rope is a deceptively easy stitch, and although it looks complex when finished, it is suitable for beginners. There are three simple rules to creating spiral rope: thread the needle from bottom to top through the core; always add a new spiral to the same side as the previous one; and pass through the same number of core beads each time.

Using size 8 for the core and size 11 outer beads for your first rope will allow you to get the hang of it quickly – then you can start experimenting!

*BELOW* Replacing the outer beads with a long bugle creates a different effect.

## HOW IT'S DONE

**1** Pick up three core and five outer beads. Pass back through the core beads and move the loop you've created so that it's covered by your thumb.

**2** Pick up one core and five outer beads and pass back through the last two core beads, plus the new one.

**3** Tuck the loop under your thumb on top of the previous one.

**4** Pass back through the previous two core beads, plus the new one, and tuck the loop under your thumb.

**5** Keep doing this until you have made the correct length of rope.

**6** There will be one loose end of thread at each end of the rope. Use this to sew on a clasp or attach to a bag, then take the thread down through the beads and tie half-hitches to secure it.

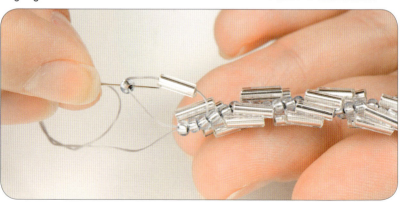

# Question 130:
# Is there a way of modifying spiral rope?

You can alter the look of spiral rope by changing the number of beads you pass through in the core, or by stepping up through the third or fourth bead instead to create a more open pattern. You can also use different beads such as drops and bugles to alter the look of your spiral cord. A variation of spiral cord known as double-core spiral makes a particularly attractive rope.

*BELOW* Join lengths of double-core spiral into loops to make a chain bracelet.

## HOW IT'S DONE

**1** Pick up two cinnamon and two blue double delicas (size 8 cylinder beads), and tie in a circle.

**2** Take the needle back through the two cinnamon again and pick up another cinnamon and blue bead.

**3** Circle the thread through the top two beads again. As you add the next two double delicas, pass the needle through two blue beads already added.

**4** Pick up a short bugle and take the needle directly across and up through the two cinnamon beads.

**5** Turn the beading over to the other side. Pick up four size 11 seed beads. These will sit diagonally across the block of four double delicas directly below where the thread emerges. Take the needle back through two double delicas.

**6** Turn the beading over and take the needle across and back through the top cinnamon bead, ready to begin the sequence again. Continue until the rope is the length required.

# Question 131:
# What is the difference between ropes and tubes?

The main difference between a tube and a rope is that a tube has a hollow center and a rope has a solid core. A rope is simply worked in your hand with a needle and thread, since it has a solid core. Tubes can be worked in your hand, but it is usually easier to work around a mandrel, which is a rod or similar implement, to help you form the tube shape cleanly.

Most bead-weaving stitches can be worked in a tube if you want, but the stitch that follows can only be worked as a tube. Dutch spiral has a really unique look to it, and it can be worked with small bugles and tiny beads, or you can swap the seed beads for crystals for a really unique effect.

## HOW IT'S DONE

**1** Pick up a seed bead, then a bugle, then a seed bead, then a bugle, and then another of each. Tie them into a circle and pass back through the first seed bead again.

**2** Pick up one seed bead and one bugle and pass through the next seed bead.

**3** Keep picking up a seed bead and a bugle and pass through the next seed bead for a few rounds. It is then easier to work if you insert a mandrel. Continue adding beads until your tube is the right length.

Because you have a hollow tube, you can thread a ribbon through it. A tube worked with long bugles will be very floppy, so it can be threaded onto a wide organza ribbon and will hang beautifully.

*BELOW* Dutch spiral on a needle.

# Question 132:
# How do I stitch in a tube?

Right-angle weave (see Question 121) is usually worked flat and joined with an extra row of beads to form a triangle tube (three rows) or a square tube (four rows). With peyote stitch (see Question 113), you can easily "zip up" a piece of even-count fabric end to end by stitching through the rows. Both herringbone and brick stitches are formed most easily on a tube by creating a tube of ladder stitch first (see Question 102), which forms a secure base. Work a length of ladder stitch that fits around your mandrel – a solid rod that fits snugly inside the beads and supports it as you stitch, making it easier to work a tube. Take the needle through the first and last beads again to create the tube shape.

**EXPERT TIP**

❝ To stitch a pattern on a large tube, use a clear plastic mandrel. Draw the pattern onto paper and slip it inside the tube. ❞

## Herringbone
Bring the thread out on top of the ladder stitch and work herringbone stitch as usual until you reach the point where you began (see Question 109). To step up for the next round, take the needle down through the ladder stitch base after the final pair; pass through the bead next to it, and then through the first herringbone bead. You can now begin the next row of herringbone stitch, remembering to step up at the end of each round.

## Brick stitch
Bring the thread out on top of the ladder stitch and work brick stitch as usual until you reach the first bead again (see Question 104). With the thread emerging from the top of the last bead, go down through the first bead and back up through the last bead. Begin the next row with two beads and continue in the usual way, stitching through the thread loops between beads.

# Question 133:
# How do I work African helix?

African helix is an extremely attractive tubular beading stitch worked around a mandrel (see Question 132). Since the tube is quite wide, you can string ribbon through the middle to make a necklace or bracelet. Always use two different beads – one will form the spiral, the other the background.

*LEFT* You can use anything as a mandrel, as long as the beads fit onto it snuggly!

# Question 134:
# How do I make a daisy necklace?

There are several different types of chain that look like seed-bead fringes, pieces of coral, or in the case of a daisy chain, a simple strand with flowers scattered along the length. It is a simple, bright chain that is very attractive, and can be made in various color combinations.

There are three sections to the chain – the stem, the petals, and the center. You can use different colors for each part of the flower, or make them all the same color. You can use a bead mix to create the stems in different shades of green or use one single color. Small center beads will need fewer petals to wrap around into the daisy shape, so experiment before you begin.

*BELOW* Delicate daisy chain makes a pretty necklace for children, or it can be attached to fabric to embellish a dress.

# Question 135:
# What is Nepal chain?

Nepal chain is an attractive seed-bead chain that looks like branched coral. There are two parts to the chain, stems and flowers, which can be worked in different colors or different tones of the same color. You can add another color, so that the chain appears to have both leaves and flowers on the stems. With this chain, the thread is visible, so choose one that matches one of the beads, or use a clear monofilament thread.

*BELOW* Using multiple colors gives this Nepal chain a spring feel, but it is equally beautiful if worked in only one or two colors.

## HOW IT'S DONE

**1** Pick up three stem beads and five flower beads. Thread the needle back through all three stem beads.

**2** Take the needle around the outside of the first stem bead and back through the top two stem beads.

**3** Pick up another three stem beads and five flower beads, pull tight, and pass the needle back through the stem beads.

**4** Thread through the first petal bead on the original flower to connect the two branches.

**5** Keep adding new branches until you have a chain of the correct length.

# Question 136:
# What is St. Petersburg chain?

St. Petersburg chain is like a freestanding fringe. It can be extended to form long dangles, or two pieces can be worked into one another to create a double-sided fringe.

The chain uses three different kinds of beads, which you can stitch in three different colors or all in the same color. There are main beads, which form the chain itself, turn beads at the end of the fringe as usual, and skip beads that perform the same function as turn beads (see Question 155), but are at the bottom of the fringe.

## EXPERT TIP

66 **Try using a long bugle bead then a seed bead as the turn bead for a decadent fringe, or drop beads and pendants as the turn beads for a more irregular look.** 99

### HOW IT'S DONE

**1** Pick up five main beads, skip the first one, and pass back through the second and third beads.

**2** Pick up a turn bead, and then pass back through the three beads of the first row.

**3** Pick up a skip bead, and then go through the two beads of the next row.

**4** Pick up another four main beads and pass back through the first two.

**5** Pick up a turn bead and thread back through three of the beads on this row.

**6** Pick up a skip bead and pass through the two beads of the next row.

**7** Continue, adding four main beads, the turn bead, and the skip bead until the chain is of the length you require.

**8** Once the chain is the right length, add a second row of chain using the same skip beads to create a doubled chain.

*BELOW* St. Petersburg chain.

**137** What is the difference between regular and pulled thread loom work?

**138** How do I set up my loom for regular work?

**139** How do I weave the beads?

**140** How do I correct mistakes in my loom work?

**141** Can I make my own patterns?

**142** What is the best way to finish the thread ends?

**143** How do I make toggles and loops?

**144** Can I make an integral buttonhole?

**145** How do I increase and decrease my loom work?

**146** How do I add a backing to my loom work?

**147** I want to display my work on the wall – what do I do?

**148** How do I set up for pulled-thread loom work?

**149** I pierced the warp – what do I do?

**150** How do I finish the pulled-thread work?

**151** Can I work a tube on a loom?

**152** Can I use wire on a bead loom?

**153** Can I add decorative edging?

**154** How do I add loops?

**155** How do I add fringe?

**156** How do I stop my fringing from sagging?

**157** Can I make a fringe as I work on the loom?

# 7

# BEAD LOOMING

The bead loom can be used to quickly create bands for bracelets, or it can be used to weave large pieces. These can be easily joined together to make a big picture.

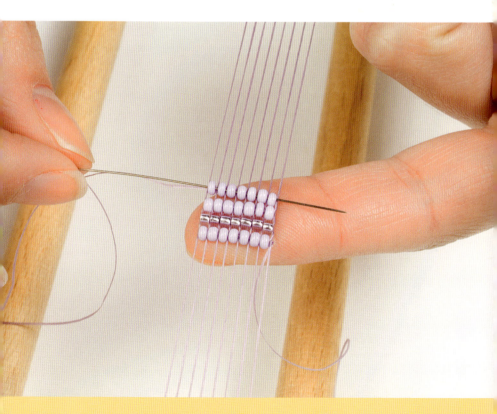

# Question 137:
# What is the difference between regular and pulled thread loom work?

All loom work requires a loom, and most looms will allow you to work using either technique. The finished fabric looks like square stitch (see Question 117), but is quicker and easier to work. Loom work is best used in place of square stitch when you are working on a large piece, as the speed at which you can bead outweighs the longer setting-up time.

In regular loom work, the loom is set up with separate warp threads. These threads provide the structure to which the other beads are attached and run down the entire length of the piece. In pulled thread, or "endless-warp" loom work, there is only one warp thread, which runs backward and forward across the loom in a zigzag pattern. When you have finished weaving, you can pull the single warp thread tight, so that there are only two thread ends to be stitched in.

The major benefit of regular loom work is that you can use any material you like for the warp threads; however, these then have to be finished in some way. Pulled thread loom work must be done with a monofilament warp thread, but it is much easier to finish the work with only two ends to weave in.

*BELOW* Beautiful examples of bead loom work on an African Market stall.

# Question 138:
# How do I set up my loom for regular work?

Count the number of beads in each row of your pattern. Each bead will have a warp thread on either side of it, so you will need a thread for each bead, plus one more. If you are working with fine thread, you may wish to add an extra thread at the sides for added strength and security. The warp threads must be at least the length of your design, plus 6 in. (15 cm) at each end for attaching to the loom and finishing once the bead work is removed from the loom.

- Knot all the threads together at one end using an overhand knot (see Question 87).
- Hook the knot onto one of the pegs on your loom. Hold the threads in one hand to tension them, and use an awl or tapestry needle to separate the threads so that there is one in each groove or coil of the spring. If you are working with beads larger than seed beads, you should space the threads to the same width as the beads.

- Use a strip of masking tape to keep the threads in the grooves, and space the threads the same distance apart at the other end of the loom, making sure the threads are not crossed.
- Tie the threads in an overhand knot and attach to the roller.
- Wind the roller to center the warps and to tension the threads, but do not overtighten.

*BELOW* Separate the threads, one into each groove, with a needle.

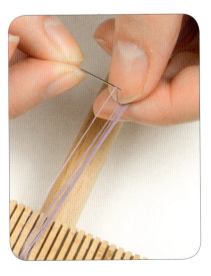

# Question 139:
## How do I weave the beads?

- Thread your needle with a long but workable length of thread, and attach it to an outer warp thread at the top of the loom.
- Pick up the first row of beads on a long beading needle and hold them under the warp threads with one bead in each gap.
- Press upward so that the holes of the beads are visible above the warp threads, and pull the needle through.
- Pass the needle back through the beads above the warp threads so that they are held securely.
- Slide the beads back and forth to check that you have not pierced the warp thread, and then pull the weft (working thread) tight.
- Pick up the next row of beads and take under the warp threads, hold in place as before, and thread the needle back through the beads. The beads should be held firmly, with the weft thread going under the warps and over the warps through each one.
- When the weft thread is 6 in. (15 cm) long, take it off the needle, and introduce a new thread to come out of the same bead. Sew in the ends with a half-hitch (see Question 89) or two once the bead work is complete.

*BELOW* Bead weaving on a loom.

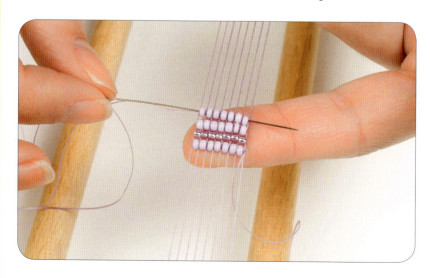

# Question 140:
# How do I correct mistakes in my loom work?

There are three common mistakes made in bead looming, and all of them are reasonably easy to fix. In a best-case scenario, you will realize that you have made a mistake when you reach the end of a row, and can easily undo your work to repair it. If you have not noticed a mistake until much later, you will have to decide whether to unpick your work or fix it using one of the methods below.

## EXPERT TIP

66 If you are working a complex pattern, stop every few rows and check back over your work. 99

| Problem | Troubleshoot | Method |
|---------|-------------|--------|
| 1 incorrect bead | Crush bead | Put a needle through the bead to prevent the thread from being cut by the breaking glass. Crush the bead from end to end with snipe- or chain-nosed pliers. Sew in a replacement bead. |
| Row missed | Insert extra row | Feed the weft thread back through the beads until there is enough slack to move the rows apart (enough to fit in the missing row). Add a new weft thread and create a new row, then weave the new weft thread in to secure it. |
| Missed warp | Re-thread beads | If you go under the warp thread when you thread the needle through the rows, the beads will drop below the level of the work when taken off the loom. You can fix this by threading a new weft through the row again, making sure it passes over the warp threads. |

# Question 141:
## Can I make my own patterns?

Bead loom work gives you a really fantastic chance to come up with your own designs and patterns. You can easily try out ideas with strips of graph paper and colored pencils, or use one of the specialist software packages to design and print your ideas from your computer. Some bead weaving design packages allow you to import pictures, which are then converted into charts for you, allowing you to weave your favorite photographs.

If you would like to create a pictorial work, you could use a section of a tapestry or cross-stitch pattern, or lay a transparent grid over a picture and color in the squares to show the shapes and colors. Simpler patterns of stripes and squares can be worked directly on the loom without a paper pattern. Because of the shape of some seed beads, the design may be shortened when worked in beads. This doesn't matter for simple shapes such as hearts, but you may have to adjust the design on graph paper to create a more realistic image.

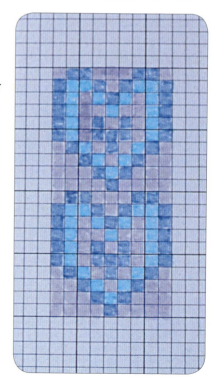

*RIGHT* Have fun experimenting with your own designs.

# Question 142:
# What is the best way to finish the thread ends?

With regular bead-loom weaving, you have the warp threads at each end and thread ends from where the weft threads have been joined down the side edges. To keep these side threads to a minimum, you should weave with as long a thread as you can. Weft ends should be threaded through one or two rows, securing them with a half-hitch (see Question 89) once or twice. Then bring them out on the surface of the beadwork rather than at the side, and trim close to the beads. Warp threads can be sewn down the length of the bracelet, although it can be tricky with so many ends to sew in. Alternatively, you can weave some warp ends across so that they come out in the center of the piece at the end, and then knot them into a calotte. You can then attach a fastening.

If you are creating a bracelet, you can use a crimp bar end to cover the warp threads. Before taking the bead work off the loom, weave the weft thread in and out of the warp threads to create a woven panel 6 mm deep. Lift off the loom and tie groups of four warp threads together with surgeons' knots (see Question 89). Trim the ends close to the knots. Attach crimp bar ends carefully to the woven ends so that the woven panel is hidden.

*BELOW* A bracelet with a crimp bar end.

# Question 143:
## How do I make toggles and loops?

Loop and toggle fastenings are a very attractive way of fastening a bracelet or choker and can be made from the same beads as you have used for the loom work. A wide band may require more than one fastening, or you can use a large bead or button for the toggle, rather than "bead raspberry" decribed below.

*RIGHT* Use one or two loop and toggle fastenings, depending on the width of the band.

### HOW IT'S DONE

**1** Sew the warp threads into the bracelet, leaving two in the middle at each end to create the fastening.

**2** At the toggle end, thread both warps onto one needle and pick up five seed beads.

**3** Pass back through three of the beads to make a small circle, and tighten the threads. This circle forms the structure the toggle is built around. Make sure there is no slack in the thread between it and the loom work.

**4** Pick up a single seed bead and pass the needle through the circle, then pick up another bead before passing the needle back through the circle.

**5** Continue adding beads, first to one side and then the other, until you have a well-rounded toggle that looks like a tiny raspberry.

**6** Take the threads down through the "stalk" and weave them into the loom work securely.

**7** To make the loop at the other end, pick up half the beads on one thread, and half on the other.

**8** Pass the needles from each strand through the beads on the other thread to create a double-threaded loop. Make sure the loop is only just big enough for the toggle so the bracelet will not slip off, and then weave the warp ends into the bracelet.

# Question 144:
# Can I make an integral buttonhole?

An integral buttonhole requires some forward planning, because you have to leave beads out in the loom work itself. The design should have an odd number of beads so that the slot can sit centrally – unless of course you are going to create more than one slot. Work two or three rows of beading before the buttonhole so that the beadwork has a firm base.

## HOW IT'S DONE

**1** Pick up enough beads to work half the width of the bracelet without picking up a bead for the central slot.

**2** Hold the beads in position under the warp threads on one side, and take the needle out through the central slot.

**3** Thread the needle back through the beads, making sure that you go around the warp thread in the center.

**4** Continue working these short half rows to the end of the buttonhole, then work back through each row to strengthen them.

**5** Pass back through the last full row of beads, and then fill in the other side of the buttonhole in the same way.

**6** Continue, adding the center bead in again to work the full width of the bracelet.

*BELOW* Make sure your buttonhole is big enough for the button!

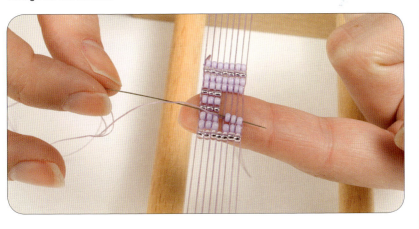

# Question 145:
# How do I increase and decrease my loom work?

Increasing and decreasing the number of beads in each row allows you to shape your loom work. You can use these techniques to shape the ends of your work into points or curves with the threads sewn in, or to create shaped medallions of beadwork where the warp threads become a feature of the design. For shaped points, you need to set up the loom with enough warp threads for the widest part of your work. It is easier to weave the wide section first and then join in a new thread to decrease at each end to create the points.

To decrease, take the needle around the warp at the end of the row and pass back through the number of beads that you want to decrease by. Go around the new outer warp thread before picking up the reduced number of beads for the next row.

To increase, pass the needle under the warp thread at the end of the row and pick up the beads that you want to increase the row by. Lay the beads on top of the warp threads and hold in position, then put the needle back through the beads, making sure it goes under the warp threads. Pick up the rest of the beads on the row, and hold them under the warp threads. Thread the needle back through on top of the warps to hold the row in place.

## EXPERT TIP

66 Use decorative warp threads in different colors, textures, and thicknesses and then leave them exposed by weaving disk or diamond shapes for a really eye-catching effect. 99

# Question 146:
# How do I add a backing to my loom work?

Adding backing to your loom work makes it stronger and harder wearing, and is a good way to hide all the warp ends. You can use any non-fray fabric, such as felt, leather, suede, or ribbon, cut to the same size as the beading.

For the best finish with backed pieces, plan the backing as part of the design process, thinking about each of the following:

- Does your piece need to fit an existing piece of ribbon or bias binding?
- Will the backing be in contact with the skin? If so, you may want to use a softer more pliable fabric.
- Does the backing need to match the warp or weft threads?
- How does the color of the backing affect the color of the piece? This will be especially noticeable with dark backing fabric and transparent beads.
- If the piece is very large, will you need to attach the backing in the center also?
- How will findings, embellishments, and frames or hanging bars be attached?
- Will the fabric be visible, for example, when adding a band of bead-loom work to a bag?

## HOW IT'S DONE

**1** First, tie the warp threads in pairs, then cut to half the length of the piece.

**2** Fold the warps down behind the piece and lay it onto the backing fabric.

**3** Choose a thread that matches your backing fabric, thread a sewing needle, and attach to the fabric with three tiny stitches. Take the needle over the warp threads back through the fabric to form an overhand stitch. Keep the stitches very small and neat, and attach the fabric to the beading all the way around by stitching through the warp threads.

## EXPERT TIP

66 If the piece is to be used as jewelry, stitch the findings directly to the fabric – if you have used felt, stitch through the warp threads to make sure the fastenings are secure. 99

# Question 147:
# I want to display my work on the wall – what do I do?

If you are creating a piece to hang on the wall, you can use the warp threads to hang it, and it can also be an extra decoration. The simplest way to do this is to knot the ends and use this to hang it on a hook. The warp threads at the bottom of the work can be strung with beads like a fringe. You can plait the warp threads at either end and form loops to hang the work, or use it as a decoration.

When you are going to use the warp threads as part of the decoration, you need to set up the loom with this in mind. Choose a suitable color and attractive thread if they are to be plaited or left as a fringe, or use a strong thread if you want to attach heavy bead fringing or tassels.

The work could be backed – be aware that the color of the backing will change the color of the beadwork unless you have used opaque beads, so try different colors for different effects. You could simply weave in all the ends and add loops at the top to hang the piece, or use the top warp threads to attach it to a hanging bar. Alternatively, for backed work, stitch a loop of thread or a jump ring onto the back of the fabric. For a more luxurious effect, add a loop of ribbon at the top of the piece for hanging, and a matching tassel at the bottom.

## EXPERT TIP

66 Glass beads are light fast – why not hang your work in front of a window or light source for a really amazing effect? You will need to think carefully about the materials you use for the warp and weft threads – natural fibers will break down in strong sunlight, and may not enjoy regular dusting! 99

# Question 148:
# How do I set up for pulled-thread loom work?

Almost any loom can be set up with a continuous thread, which can either be worked and finished as standard weaving or, if you have been careful not to pierce the warp, it can be eased through the work so that there are only two warp threads to weave in. This is called pulled-thread work, and the key to successfully weaving in this way is to use a monofilament thread for the warp, which helps to prevent you from piercing it during weaving.

The first step is to decide on the number of warps needed – this will be one more than the number of beads in the widest row. Tie the warp to the peg at the end of the loom, then find the central groove on the loom. Count the grooves across to find where the first warp will be, and lay the thread through the groove. Take the thread up to the corresponding groove at the other end of the loom, lay it in, and then take it around the peg at that end. Take the thread through the next groove, and then back to the other end of the loom, through the matching groove and around the peg. Repeat until you have all the warp threads in place, and then tie the warp firmly in place.

## EXPERT TIP

66 **Rub the tip of the needle on sandpaper to dull it before weaving the beads.** 99

*LEFT* An example of pulled-thread loom work.

# Question 149:
# I pierced the warp – what do I do?

If you have pierced the warp on the row you have just finished, unthread the needle and carefully draw the weft thread out. You should be able to re-thread the needle and continue on easily. If you pierced the warp some time previously, work out which end of the weft thread is closest to the pierced warp and undo the weaving until you correct the mistake, then rework the piece.

The best way to prevent the warp from becoming pierced is to use a monofilament thread or braided thread such as Powerpro or Fireline rather than multifilament threads like Nymo or S-Lon when setting up the loom. If you cannot use monofilament thread – for example, if you are using decorative cord or ribbon and shaping in the weave – then you can remove the point of your needle with fine sandpaper or a cup bur.

After each row, slide the beads up and down the warp to check that the warp is not pierced, or weave 5 mm above the work, then slide the beads up or down to the main work when you finish each row.

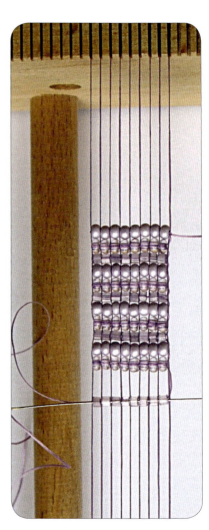

*ABOVE* before pulling the needle through, slide the beads down a little to check the warp isn't pierced.

# Question 150:
## How do I finish the pulled-thread work?

Bead your work, making sure that you don't pierce the warp threads. Take your work off the loom and lay it out on a flat surface.

- Put masking tape over the beads to help hold them in place as you tease the warp threads through.
- Start at one end of the work in the center, and gently pull the warp thread all the way through the work.
- At the other end, pull the next warp thread so that the loop you have just created is drawn up and through the work.
- Continue, alternating from end to end until you reach the end of the beadwork with only one warp thread.
- Return to the center of the work, and feed the remaining warp threads through in the same way until you reach the other side.
- Weave the threads back through the beads to secure them. If you find that you have pierced a warp thread, leave it and continue on – you will be left with one extra thread to weave in.

*RIGHT* Carefully pull the warp thread through the work.

# Question 151:
# Can I work a tube on a loom?

There are two ways of working a tube on a loom – you can work a flat piece and then weave the warp threads into the opposing ends to create a tube, or you can use a specifically designed loom to make a tube. Tube looms are usually made of clear acrylic and are threaded with a continuous warp. They are available in various sizes and have a horseshoe cross-section. You set up the tube loom by tying the warp securely to the anchor hole at one side of the loom and wrapping the thread once around the loom.

- Take the thread under the first strand and tie several half-hitch knots to secure it.
- Wrap the thread around the loom and secure with a half-hitch.

- Continue across the loom until you have one thread for each bead in the row, plus one extra. Each warp should be secured by a half-hitch, and the end of the warp secured with several half-hitches.
- Weave as usual to fill the gap in the loom, then snip the anchor thread and squeeze the loom gently to allow the beadwork to slip around.
- Continue beading until the gap is filled again, and repeat.
- When the tube is completely covered, weave the weft through the next few rows to secure, and slide the work off the tube.

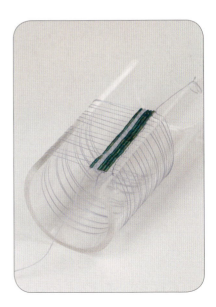

*RIGHT* Using a shaped loom makes working a tube easy; constantly turn the work so that you are always working over the gap.

# Question 152:
## Can I use wire on a bead loom?

Using wire on a bead loom allows you to create pieces that will hold their shape. You could create a tall container or a coiled decoration.

It is easier to use wire for the warp threads – this allows you to use thicker wire and smaller beads. If you use wire for the weft threads, you will have to use beads with much larger holes and very thin wire, which is more likely to break under pressure.

Use a thicker wire for the two edge warps if you want to shape the piece, and use brightly colored thread and wires for a striking effect at the edges of the beadwork. Using wires for the warp threads and creating circles or diamonds with increases and decreases allows you to add beads to the warp threads for a looser effect, with plenty of structure. You could even use memory wire for the outer warps on a tube loom to create a cuff bracelet.

*RIGHT* Create pretty Christmas decorations with your loom work.

# Question 153:
# Can I add decorative edging?

You can either add an edging to the threads on the outer edge of the beadwork, or pass the needle right through the loom work from side to side. Brick-stitch edging is worked into the warp threads and, on casual inspection, looks the same as the rest of the beading work, so it can be used to extend your work width-wise if your loom is not wide enough, or if you make a mistake with the number of rows for a pattern.

### Brick-stitch edging

- Begin with a piece of finished bead-loom work, with the warp and weft threads sewn in. Attach a new thread and bring out at the side of the beadwork, then pick up two beads on the needle.
- Take the needle under the warp thread, then take it back through the second bead. Both beads should now lie flat along the side of the beadwork.
- Pick up one bead, go under the warp thread and back through the bead again, and repeat until you reach the end of the beadwork.

### Picot edging

Picot edging is worked through the rows of beads, and gives a pretty zigzag effect along the edges of the beadwork.

- Begin with a piece of finished beadwork and take a new thread through the first row of beads.
- Pick up three beads and take the needle down through the next bead along.
- Bring the needle up through the bead next to it and pick up another three beads, and take the needle down through the next bead.

*BELOW* Adding a picot edging.

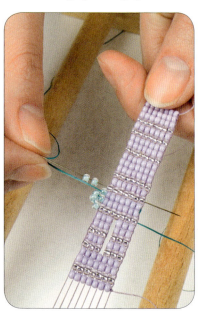

# Question 154:
# How do I add loops?

Loops can be used to add a variety of textured effects to your work. Each loop is worked by taking a new thread through a row of the beadwork, and then picking up a number of extra beads before taking it back through the beadwork to create a loop. You can create diverse effects by placing the ends of the loops in different positions.

## Semicircular looped edges

Simple semicircular looped edges can be made by picking up several beads and taking the needle through a bead, one or two rows away from where the thread emerged. You can create a simple flat edging by working loops side-by-side or overlap the loops for a more textured edging by working a back stitch before picking up beads for the next loop.

## Closed-looped edges

Closed-looped edges can be worked by taking the thread back through the original beads, creating a small teardrop shape. If you take the needle back through two beads, then move to the next row and repeat, you can create a bulky looped fringe.

## Top loops

You can also create loops on top of your bead-loom work by picking up beads and taking the needle through a few of the beads on the next row, then picking up more beads for the next loop. If you come out at the edge of the beadwork, the loops create a ridge down the side of your work.

*RIGHT* This bracelet has a row of loops worked down the center to make a ridge.

# Question 155:
# How do I add fringe?

The turn bead is the bead at the bottom of a strand of fringing, which lies horizontally and is used to turn the thread around to return through the previous beads. The turn bead could be a larger bead, a disk, or a tiny seed bead under a much larger focus bead. Fringing can be worked on its own along a length of fabric or ribbon, or can be incorporated into bead-loom work.

- To work a simple fringe on a piece of finished beadwork, take a new thread through a row of beads, pick up the number of beads you want to use for the main fringe, then pick up the turn bead.
- Pass back through all the beads except the turn bead to make the strand.
- Pass through one bead of the weaving, then back through the bead next to it to begin another strand.

*BELOW* Working a fringe on the loom.

# Question 156:
# How do I stop my fringing from sagging?

Fringing can loosen up over time and leave gaps between the beadwork and the fringe beads. It is better to prevent this from happening in the first place than try to fix it later. Use a thread with as little stretch in it as possible, and then stretch it before you begin to ensure that there is no "give" at all. To stretch threads and cord, unwind the length you will need, plus a little extra just in case, and thread some large stone or glass beads onto it. Tie the ends together and hang overnight – if you decide to use a different thread, you will still have a piece of stretched thread to use next time.

It is a good idea to make your fringe slightly stiffer than you want it; this will allow the fabric you are stitching to move to accommodate the weight of the fringe. Make sure you pull the thread tight after each strand, as it is very difficult to tighten the single strands afterward.

Tightly packed fringe may have a slightly different problem – the fringes may not lie straight, but move and get tangled. To help keep them straight, put a heavier bead above the turn bead on every other strand to encourage them to fall back into position.

*BELOW* Use a heavier bead at the end of the fringing to encourage the strands to remain straight.

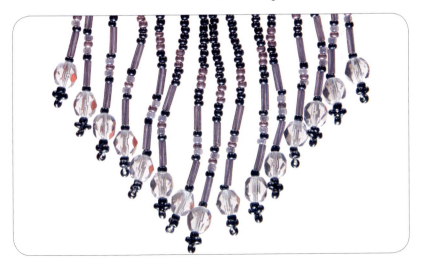

# Question 157:
# Can I make a fringe as I work on the loom?

It is possible to work fringing at the same time as weaving by picking up the fringe beads on the end of the weft thread as you work each row. This prevents you from having to go through the beads over and over again, which is helpful if you're using ordinary seed beads with small holes.

- To work a fringe at the same time as your loom work, pick up the fringe beads after you pick up the looming beads on the same thread.
- Leave the turn bead and pass back through the rest of the fringe beads
- Hold the beads up between the warp threads and take the needle back through the holes above the warp.
- Add the next row in the same way.

You can also work fringing in the middle of a piece of beadwork to create a vertical fountain of beads. This can be done by adding a thread in the center of the work and working fringing as normal, or by adding the fringe as you work.

- Weave a few rows on the loom, then pass back through a few of the beads in the last row, bring the needle out, and create a strand of fringe.
- Take the needle back into the work and through more beads on the row.
- Add more strands until you finish this row, add another row of beads, then fringe afterward in the same way.

*BELOW* Making a fringe on the loom.

*LEFT* Fringing can be used to accessorize almost anything!

**158** What is the best way to cut wire?

**159** How do I make jump rings?

**160** How do I make simple loops?

**161** How do I open and close findings and jump rings?

**162** Can I make my own ear wires?

**163** How do I wire a hanging pendant?

**164** How do I make a double-hook-and-eye finding?

**165** What is a closed-loop chain?

**166** How do I add chain to my jewelry?

**167** What can I do to add texture to chain?

**168** What is chain maille?

**169** Can I add beads to chain maille?

**170** How do I make my own chain?

**171** What is a zigzag spacer?

**172** How do I use a jig?

**173** Why is my twisted wire uneven?

**174** Is it possible to knit with wire?

**175** How do I make a wire ribbon tube?

**176** Can I crochet with wire?

**177** How do I make a spiral cage?

**178** How do I wrap a drop bead?

**179** Can I wrap a bead in wire?

**180** How else can I use wrapping to add texture?

**181** How do I make coils?

**182** Can I vary the shapes of coils?

**183** How do I add texture to my coils?

**184** How do I make wire spirals?

**185** How do I create spiral beads?

# 8

# WIREWORK

Wire comes in many colors, thicknesses, and finishes. You can form it into specialized findings and create an endless variety of shapes and textures.

# Question 158:
# What is the best way to cut wire?

You should always use wire cutters rather than scissors for cutting wire, as you will damage the blades. Use heavy-duty cutters for memory wire, as the wire is so hard that it will damage normal cutters. Side cutters are the most suitable for jewelry because the blades have a flat side and a slanted side.

- When you are cutting wire, make sure the flat side is toward your work in order to get a flat end on the wire. This is essential when making your own jump rings so that the ends butt together.
- Keep your fingers away from the blades while cutting the wire, and take care to prevent a piece from springing up into your face. When cutting, turn the blades so that the waste will be thrown downward and away from you.
- Collect any scraps and store larger pieces for later use. Even tiny pieces of pure silver can be kept for recycling.
- Wire ends can be filed to smooth any rough edges. Hold the wire close to the end when filing so that you do not bend or kink it. Use a cup burr to round the end of wires when making your own earwires.

*LEFT* Wire cutters are the safest and most efficient tool for dealing with wire.

# Question 159:
# How do I make jump rings?

Although you can buy jump rings in common sizes and metallic colors, if you are working with a more unusual chain or wire, you may need to make your own jump rings. This will be particularly useful if you want to create colored rings or nonstandard-size rings for chain maille.

It is easy to make a few jump rings using basic round-nose pliers or standard sizes using three-step pliers, but you will find it easier to make larger numbers by winding wire on a knitting needle or similar rod.

• Wind a length of wire around the knitting needle to make a tight spiral. You will need to wrap the wire several more times than the number of jump rings required.

• Remove the knitting needle and open the coils slightly by pulling each end.

• Cut the end straight for the first ring.

• Turn the wire cutters and cut again directly above the first cut. Turn the cutters to trim the end and then repeat the process to make as many jump rings as required. In this way, you make two flat ends so that the jump rings close completely, making your jewelry more secure.

*BELOW* Cut carefully so that the loops do not shoot off!

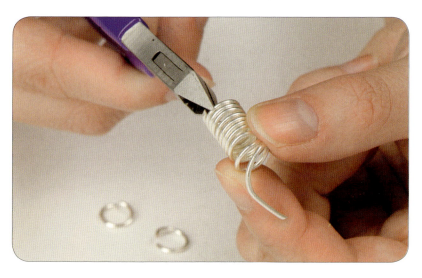

# Question 160:
# How do I make simple loops?

Creating simple loops is an essential skill in jewelry making – loops hold your work together, allowing you to link elements easily. A loop on the end of a wire is essentially an eye pin, which you can thread with beads and secure with a crimp, or more attractively, by making a small loop or coil. Forming a simple loop on either side of a bead creates a bead link; this can then be added into a piece of chain to add texture.

Begin by holding the very end of a piece of wire in your round-nose pliers. If you run your finger over the pliers, you should only just be able to feel the tip of the wire between the jaws.

- Turn the pliers gently toward you, holding the wire close to the jaws

with your thumb. You will need to open the pliers slightly and move the wire around in order, then turn the end toward you again to get a completely smooth loop.

- Once the tip of the wire meets the main wire again, reposition the pliers in the loop and bend the wire back slightly so that the eye is directly above the wire itself.

- If your loop is too small, begin further down the round-nose pliers; if it is too big, hold the wire closer to the tip.

*BELOW* Bend the wire a little at a time to get a smooth loop.

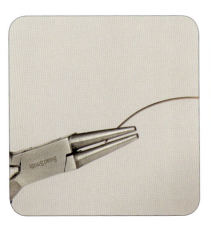
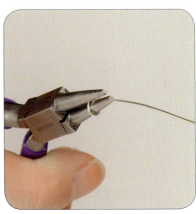

# Question 161:
## How do I open and close findings and jump rings?

When opening any loop, whether it is a jump ring, an eye pin, or a bought finding, you should always use the same technique.

- Hold each side of the loop with a pair of flat-nose pliers, trying to cover as much of the ring as possible to prevent it from twisting out of shape.
- Bring one hand toward you, twisting gently so that the loop opens with the ends still in line. Do not pull the ends apart out of the circular shape, as you will not be able to return it to its perfect loop.
- To close the loop, hold with two pairs of pliers as before and carefully ease the loop back into shape. Always use flat-nose pliers with no serrations to avoid damaging the metal.
- Once you have re-closed a jump ring, there may be a larger gap between the two ends than before. To close the gap, hold the ring as if you are going to open it and then open and close several times, putting pressure on the pliers so that the ends come together. This technique will also cause the wire to harden and strengthen the rings.
- If you want to make sure the ends butt together so that it is more secure, you can use pliers to ease the ends of the rings so that they overlap slightly, then back again to the closed position. This will tension the ring and hold it more tightly in place.

*LEFT* Pull apart the ends of the jump ring with pliers.

# Question 162:
## Can I make my own ear wires?

Fishhook findings are easy to make, so you can create your own with an individual twist to complement your earrings. If you are not allergic to metal you can use a wider variety of materials – try bright, color-coated wires with silver beads, or copper wires with bright blue. Creating your own fishhooks also allows you to include twisted wire embellishments, or matching beads above the eye (see also Question 26).

### HOW IT'S DONE

**1** Cut a piece of wire at least 1.5 in. (4 cm) long and make a small loop in one end with round-nose pliers. This will be the eye loop to attach the rest of the earring to.

**2** Hold the wire with flat-nose pliers; the loop needs to be perpendicular to the jaws and flush against them.

**3** Bend the wire at right angles, then hold with the widest part of your round-nose pliers and bend into a hook.

**4** Trim the wire to the right length and bend the end up slightly to help stop the wires from slipping out of your ear.

**5** Carefully round the end of the wire with a cup burr to smooth any rough edges.

**6** Add beads between the loop and hook – for a luxurious effect, use a crystal.

## EXPERT TIP

**❝ Half-round pliers are specialist pliers that make it much easier to bend wire into curved shapes when making ear wires. ❞**

# Question 163:
# How do I wire a hanging pendant?

Large disks and flat shapes with holes from front to back make beautiful pendants, but you may find it difficult to obtain pendant findings to fit. You can create your own findings using a wrapped loop.

- Thread the wire through the pendant and bend the wire gently around it, leaving a long tail.
- Leave some space to allow the pendant to move without damaging the wire, and wrap the tail around the other wire two or three times to make a tight spiral. Trim the tail close to the spirals.
- For a more ornate effect, you can add a small bead to the main wire before forming a loop to join the pendant to a necklace. If the pendant is heavy, make a wrapped loop again.
- Leave a small gap before bending the wire into a loop around your round-nose pliers.
- After creating the loop, hold it firmly with flat-nose pliers, then wind the tail end of the wire around the main wire two or three times to hold the loop closed.
- Trim as before and string the pendant on a cord or chain.

*BELOW* Wrapped loops were used to secure the beads on this key ring.

# Question 164:
# How do I make a double-hook-and-eye finding?

A double-hook-and-eye only has a single eye and a single hook. The name comes from the fact that the wire used is doubled for strength and security. Both parts of the finding have a bead for decoration that also separates the wrapped wire ends. You could use small metal beads to match the wire, or beads that match those in the necklace.

- Cut a long length of wire and wind it around round-nose pliers to make a loop about 1 in. (2.5 cm) from the end.
- Hold the wire loop tightly in flat-nose pliers and then twist the short end two or three times around the long wire to secure it.
- Trim off the excess and thread a bead onto the wire.

- Hold the wire with the tip of the round-nose pliers and bend the wire back on itself.
- Twist the end wire two or three times to hold the doubled-over length together and the bead tightly in place.
- Use nylon-coated pliers to smooth the doubled wires, and then use round-nose pliers to form the doubled wire into a hook with a bent back tip.

*LEFT* Use a double-hook-and-eye finding for an extra secure fastening.

# Question 165:
# What is a closed-loop chain?

A closed loop chain is made up of lots of bead links made with wrapped loops that are all joined together and cannot be pulled apart. This is the technique used to create Rosary beads. Each link in the chain is made in exactly the same way as the first. However, you have to form them linked, which makes it slightly trickier.

- Choose the beads for the link and cut a piece of wire the same length plus an extra 2.5 in. (6 cm). Each bead link will require a piece of wire the same length.
- Create a loop in the wire with round-nose pliers, and hold it with snipe-nose pliers while you twist the short end around the main wire two or three times. Thread the beads onto the wire and create another loop, and twist the loose end of wire to hold the beads in place. Trim off the excess.
- Form a loop in the next piece of wire with the round-nose pliers, and slip the previous link into the loop before you twist the wire to close it.
- Add the beads, then finish with another twisted loop.
- Continue in the same way, linking each one to the previous link as you make it.

*BELOW* Use snipe-nose pliers while you twist the short end.

# Question 166:
# How do I add chain to my jewelry?

Chain gives a professional look to your jewelry. It is available in many colors, materials, shapes, and sizes, and can be bought in packs or by the foot, like ribbon. It is a good idea to make sure you can buy findings and wire to match when you buy unusual chain, as you may find it tricky to match later.

- Chain is usually formed from open links, with only the more expensive having soldered links. You can use ordinary wire cutters to cut chain cutting through one side of the link, or as you would separate jump rings, unless they are soldered where you will need to cut through both sides. When you measure chain, lay it flat next to a ruler and cut the next link with the tip of your pliers.
- Connect chain to findings or bead links using jump rings – open the jump ring with two pairs of pliers, and slip the end of the chain or the finding loop inside before closing the jump ring again.
- If you are hanging charms and pendants from chain, lay the chain out flat, and attach them all to the same side of the chain; this allows the charms to hang attractively.

*BELOW* Use chain in your jewelry to create a professional look.

# Question 167:
# What can I do to add texture to chain?

There are several ways of adding texture to chain. You can add headpin dangles using matching wires and subtle beads to create a sense of texture without being overwhelming. You can add ribbon through, or wound around, the links, which gives the chain added softness and color. You can also scrunch the chain up to create an attractive crinkly texture.

## Thread onto ribbon

- Try different widths and materials such as satin or organza ribbons for a variety of effects.
- Thread the ribbon onto a large-eyed needle, and weave evenly back and forth through the links.
- Leave a long tail of ribbon at either end and lay it out flat, adjusting the lie of the chain.
- To secure the ribbon neatly, thread the ribbon through a large tube crimp and a jump ring and back through the crimp.
- Thread the ribbon through the last link of the chain and back through the crimp.
- Tighten the ribbon until the last link and jump ring are tight up against the crimp.

- Squeeze the crimp to flatten it and then repeat at the other end.
- Cut off any excess ribbon.

## Threads onto elastic

You can also thread chain onto elastic, allowing the links to fold up together, almost as if you have threaded lots of jump rings together. This is a highly textured use of chain, which scrunches up irregularly to create a wide and random cluster of loops. You can use this on its own to create an elasticized bracelet, add charms, or even thread the elasticized chain onto memory wire to create a textured cuff bracelet.

*BELOW* Cluster up the chain on elastic for a highly textured effect.

# Question 168:
# What is chain maille?

Chain maille is made by linking metal rings to create a flexible fabric. It was originally used to make a protective garment for soldiers, and its strength and durability makes it a good choice for small pouches and bags. There are various styles of chain maille. Japanese chain maille, which makes an attractive fabric, is formed by linking rings at 90-degree angles; small rings are used to link larger rings together, forming smooth and attractive fabric. You can also use small sections to create small motifs.

As the small rings need to fit snugly around the larger rings, you may want to create your own larger rings with thicker wire. As an alternative, you can double the large rings as well as the smaller ones. To make Japanese chain maille:

- Connect two large rings with two small jump rings set side by side.
- Lay the two large rings side by side, and add a third large ring to one side with two small rings.
- Create two chains in the same way, and then lay one below the other so that the large rings fit closely together.
- Add pairs of small rings to link the two rows of rings, laying the maille out flat between and adding each pair to ensure that the fabric does not get twisted.

*LEFT* Various samples of chain maille.

# Question 169:
# Can I add beads to chain maille?

There are a number of ways that you can add beads to chain maille. The easiest is to add one or more tiny beads to the jump rings before you connect them. This technique is suitable for flat chain maille techniques such as Japanese chain maille. It is easy to create a flat cuff-style bracelet with a pretty beaded border. More advanced beading techniques trap beads inside one of the more ornate chain maille ropes such as Byzantine chain maille. You can also add larger beads between sections of chain maille using a closed or open bead link.

*BELOW* Beaded Japanese chain maille.

# Question 170:
# How do I make my own chain?

Creating simple chain with jump rings linked together individually is not very effective, as the resulting chain does not lie very well and the rings can be pulled apart with relatively little force. On the other hand, chains formed with more than one ring used for each link are very striking and very strong. There are lots of ways to link jump rings to make different chain maille designs. You can form long chains with simple multiples of two or three rings in each link, or use particular techniques such as using Byzantine or Persian chain maille to create a very ornate chain that is attractive enough to wear as a necklace or bracelet without further ornamentation.

This simple chain is called flower chain, as it is formed by creating "flowers" of interlinked jump rings, which are then joined together with single jump rings to make a chain.

- Create the individual "flowers" by joining two jump rings, then placing one on top of the other.
- Add a third ring by looping it through the intersection point of the previous two. This should form a close weave of rings – if one appears to stick out, flip it over so that the rings sit snugly together.
- Use single jump rings to connect your flowers into a long chain – make sure you join them through the center of the flower, not through a single petal.

*BELOW* Make your own chain using multiple rings.

# Question 171:
# What is a zigzag spacer?

A zigzag spacer (zigzag connector or link) is a spectacularly shaped piece of wire that can be used between bead links to create a fantastic chain, or added as a dangle or charm to chain and strung beads. You can make the zigzag spacers by hand using round-nose pliers, or more easily on a wire jig.

- Cut the wires to the same length before you begin, and measure one against the other until you have created a set that matches – they will not be identical, but a good match is very attractive.
- Use your round-nose pliers to create a loop in the end of the wire, and then bend the end out to the

side of the loop.
- Hold the wire in round-nose pliers a little along from the loop and bend it back upon itself. Move along the wire and bend it around the pliers again.
- Bend the wire backward and forward into an attractive rounded zigzag.
- When it is shaped as you'd like, add another loop to match the first. Use these loops to attach the zigzag as a charm or as a link in a chain.

*BELOW* Using a jig creates perfectly matched zigzag spacers (see also Question 172).

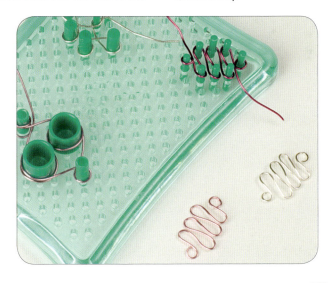

# Question 172:
# How do I use a jig?

A wire jig is used to form loops and other filigree patterns with wire. It is made up of a base with evenly spaced holes and a number of pegs of various sizes. The pegs can be fitted into the holes in any pattern, and wire can be bent and twisted around them to create delicate pieces. You can use pegs that are all the same size, or use different sizes to make big and small loops.

If you leave the pegs in position, you can make identical pieces of wirework over and over again. This makes a jig particularly useful for creating filigree earrings, where a perfectly matched pair is necessary. You can also draw out the pattern, or take a quick photo reference so that you can recreate the same piece at a later date.

- Wind wire closely around the pegs, making sure that the loops are flat on the base. Use a knitting needle to press them down if necessary.
- To get the wire off the jig, either lift it carefully with pliers, or if it is very complex and delicate, remove the pegs while carefully holding the wire flat.

*BELOW* A wire jig is useful if you wish to create identical patterns.

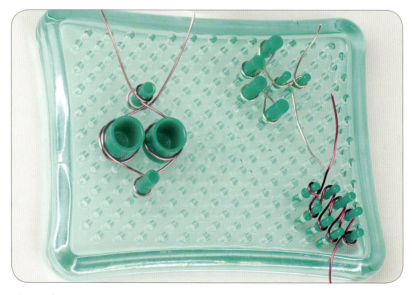

# Question 173:
# Why is my twisted wire uneven?

Twisting wires by hand creates an uneven spiral in the wire, as you are unable to use completely even pressure all the way along the twist. It is easier to create an even twist if you pass it through a bead, which helps you hold it more easily for twisting. You can create small amounts of smoothly twisted wire by rolling the bead between your fingers in one hand while holding the other end with the ends spread apart with your other hand.

- To create branched wirework, add a bead to one of the wires for each extra branch.
- After making a branch, twist from the original bead to continue the stalk.

To create long lengths of evenly twisted wire, you will need more equipment. A cord maker or a hand drill with a hook mounted in the chuck is ideal.

- Fold the wire in half and put the folded end over the hook, then trap the other end in a vice or have someone else hold it with pliers.
- Turn the handle smoothly until you create the desired effect. Keep the wire taut as you twist for a really smooth finish, but take care as you release the wire, as it may spring back.

## EXPERT TIP

66 Even if you don't have a drill or a cord maker you can still make long lengths of evenly twisted wire. Fold the wire in half and tuck a pencil in the loop. Secure the cut ends in a vice or have someone hold the pliers. Hold the wires loosely in your fist and turn the pencil around and around with a finger on your other hand until the wire is twisted to the desired effect. 99

# Question 174:
## Is it possible to knit with wire?

Knitting with wire is very different from knitting with yarn, but ironically it is easier for a beginner knitter to knit with wire than an accomplished knitter used to knitting firmly tensioned yarn.

When knitting with wire, the stitches are kept reasonably loose, as there is no stretch in wire. To get a smooth finish, knit with an even tension, as you cannot tighten the stitches later. You do not need to use fancy stitches when knitting with wire – just cast on, knit a panel of garter or stocking stitch, and cast off. The beauty in wire knitting is achieved by adding beads rather than creating ribs or other textures with different stitches.

The wire needs to be 28 or 32 swg (see Question 59) so that it is thin enough to knit with, but not so thin that it will snap. As with yarn knitting, leave the wire as a continuous length.

**Adding beads:**

- Knit without beads to begin with, and do not worry if it looks tangled and messy – wire knitting needs to be pulled into shape afterward to achieve its true beauty.
- Once you are feeling confident, thread some seed beads onto the wire – let them slide down to the coil and leave them alone until you have knitted a few rows.
- Knit the first stitch of the next row as normal, then pick up a few beads and hold them in the palm of your hand.
- As you knit the next stitch, push a bead up behind the needles as you bring the wire around. This will trap the bead in the stitch.
- Knit a bead into every stitch except the last one on the row.
- Knit the next row without adding any beads. Alternate between beaded and plain rows to create an attractive beaded fabric.

*BELOW* Knitting with wire is fun, but is very different from knitting with yarn.

# Question 175:
## How do I make a wire ribbon tube?

Knitted tubes are made using a technique called French knitting (or spool knitting). The knitting is created on a cylinder with pegs at the top. When cotton reels were wooden, you could make a knitting nancy or jenny by hammering four panel pins into the top; now you can buy the tool that often looks a little like a person or you can buy mechanized tools that have a turning handle to create a wire tube in double quick time. You can also buy larger cylinders or rings with more pegs to make a wider diameter tube.

- To begin, feed the tail down through the hole in the knitting nancy.
- Take the wire around the back of the first pin and across the front of that pin and the adjacent pin.
- Repeat to wrap the wire around each pin.
- To begin knitting, wrap the wire around the first pin again in the same way.
- Using a tapestry needle, gently lift the bottom loop over the top loop.
- Wrap the wire around the next pin and lift the bottom loop over again.
- Continue until the ribbon tube is the required length.

*RIGHT* Turn the crank of the knitting machine to create your knitted tube.

# Question 176:
# Can I crochet with wire?

Crocheting with wire is as easy as crocheting with yarn, but it does damage your crochet hook, so you should use inexpensive tools. You generally use a much larger hook in relation to the thickness of the wire than you would with yarn, as the wire doesn't stretch, and so you need to create larger loops. The simplest wire crochet technique is a single chain, made by working single crochet over and over again. If you string beads onto the wire before beginning, you can add a bead with every stitch. The bead can be added between the stitches or as you work the stitch. Experiment to find what looks better with your particular beads; tiny, semiprecious chips are particularly effective.

Cuff-style bracelets and chokers can be made using filet crochet techniques. This simple technique generally uses blocks of treble worked along a foundation chain. You then work backward and forward to create the desired pattern of blocks and gaps. Circular shapes are also easy to work with wire crochet. Chain five or six stitches and make into a ring. Work ten or twelve double or treble stitches into the ring. On the next round, work two stitches, either double or treble, into each stitch to keep a flat shape.

*BELOW* Plait single crochet chains with faux suede make an attractive bracelet.

# Question 177:
# How do I make a spiral cage?

A spiral cage will hold an oval or round bead securely in a spiral of wire so that you can add it to wirework jewelry or chain. Experiment with different lengths of wire to create tighter or looser spirals – for a 0.5 in. (1.5 cm) diameter bead you will need approximately 8 in. (20 cm) of wire (see also Question 181).

- Hold the wire end in a pair of round-nose pliers and bend it gently around the tip of the pliers to create a u-shape.
- Hold the bead carefully in flat-nose pliers and carefully bend the wire around to begin the spiral.
- Move the spiral in the pliers often so that the wire curves around to create a smooth tight spiral.
- Once you have coiled half the wire, bend the other end into a u-shape and coil it in the opposite direction to create an s-shaped spiral.

- Put the tip of the round-nose pliers into the hole in the center of each spiral and gently push down on the spiral to create domes.
- Fold the spiral over to create a cage and enclose the bead within it.
- Thread an eye-pin through the holes in the spiral and the bead-hole, and create a loop at the top to hang the bead cage from.

*BELOW* Experiment with spiral cages in your jewelry designs.

# Question 178:
# How do I wrap a drop bead?

Both pendant and drop beads can be given a wire-wrapped fastening to attach them to your jewelry. A small pendant bead with a wrapped cap can be hung from a chain as an attractive charm, or a large semiprecious stone can be used as a pendant.

*RIGHT* Drop beads and pendants come in all sorts of shapes and sizes.

## HOW IT'S DONE

**1** Thread a long headpin through the center of the bead so that the head supports the bottom of the bead.

**2** Leave a short stalk, and then bend the wire into a small loop with round-nose pliers.

**3** Hold the loop in flat-nose pliers, and wrap the loose wire down around the stalk and over the top of the bead.

**4** Either trim the loose end, or create a small decorative loop to lie flat against the side of the bead.

**Drop beads with horizontal holes are more delicate than pendant beads and must be hung on a length of wire.**

**1** Put a piece of wire through the hole of the bead, and carefully bend the wires so that they cross above the bead.

**2** Bend one with flat-nose pliers above the crossover so that it points directly upward, and then wrap the other wire around it in a tight spiral.

**3** Cut the wire closely and then bend the other wire into a loop and cut off the excess.

# Question 179:
## Can I wrap a bead in wire?

Wrapping a single large bead in wire allows you to create a unique pendant or focus bead. It can turn a large, plain glass bead into a really eye-catching feature very easily, and there are lots of variations you can add to this simple technique for even greater impact.

- Make a small loop with round-nose pliers in strong wire, and then hold the loop with flat-nose pliers and twist the tail of the wire around the stem two or three times. This loop will sit at the bottom of the bead, so it does not have to be large – just big enough to prevent the wire from slipping through the hole.
- Cut a length of thinner wire at least twelve times the length of the bead, and create a tiny spiral in the end of it with round-nose pliers just big enough to slip onto the other wire.
- Feed the short wire through the spiral, then the bead. The spiral will now sit inside the hole of the bead (out of sight).
- Wind the long wire around the bead until you reach the other end,

and then twist it tightly around the core wire in a spiral.
- Cut off the excess wrapping wire and add a small bead.
- Create a loop just above the bead with round-nose pliers, wrap the loose wire two or three times to close, then trim the excess.
- Using snipe-nose pliers or the corner of flat-nose pliers, twist the wire wrapped around the bead to form kinks – this will add texture and tighten the wire.

*RIGHT* This beautiful watch has glass beads wrapped in silver wire to form an elegant strap.

# Question 180:
# How else can I use wrapping to add texture?

In addition to wrapping a single bead with a single wire, you can wrap your bead with multiple wires in different colors and thicknesses. The wrapping wires can be twisted together before you wind them around the bead – for an eye-catching effect, twist a thin, colored wire around a thicker silver wire before you wrap it around the bead.

You can also thread small beads onto the wrapping wires and use the tightening kinks to hold them in place – these will catch the light differently to the wires and base bead.

You can also wind wire around strands of beads. Thread the beads onto memory wire or stiff bead threading wire so that they will hold their shape against the wire wrapping. The effect of the wire wrapping will be heightened if you scatter beads of the same color as the wire among the strung beads, and use findings that match it. Attach the wrapping wire to one strand and wind it around the other strands. Add beads to the wrapping wire as you go – if you add them only to one side, then you will have a flat surface to rest against the skin.

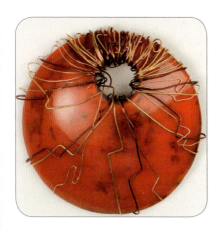

*LEFT* Make your pendant particularly eye catching by wrapping the bead in wire.

# Question 181:
# How do I make coils?

The secret to coiling wire is patience. Tight coils need a good pair of round-nose pliers with small tips to make the initial loop, and a pair of smooth-jawed flat-nose pliers to continue turning the coils tightly.

- Hold the length of wire by the very tip, in the very end of the round-nose pliers, and bend it into a u-shape.
- Hold the u-shape in the round-nose pliers tightly and bend the wire slightly to continue the coil.
- Move the coil to the flat-nose pliers and continue bending. Each time, you should only be adding a few mm of wire to the coil – if you try to add more, it will lose the smooth lines. For an even but loose coil use the round-nose pliers throughout.
- Create a full loop on the tip of the pliers, then reposition the coil so that you can wrap around the pliers again to continue.
- Keep moving the pliers around the coil, bending the wire by tiny amounts to create a completely smooth coil.

*BELOW* Gently bend the wire into a coil using your flat-nose pliers.

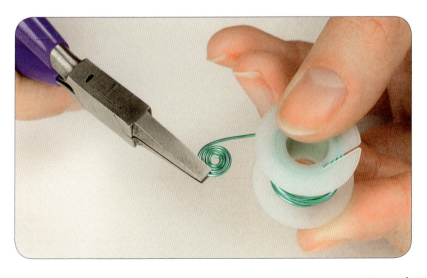

# Question 182:
## Can I vary the shapes of coils?

By simply starting the coil at the base of the round-nose pliers, you can create a completely different effect with your coil – a large round hole with tight coils around it is created in the same way as a smaller coil but looks entirely different. You can also vary the size by adding more coils, or make tiny coils with only two or three layers to fit under a shaped bead.

By moving the coil varying amounts in the flat-nose pliers, you can achieve a much more random, much looser feel. You can also create a circular center for your coil, and then change the shape of the outer coils, bending them into entirely different shapes using flat- and round-nose pliers. Flower, star, and square shapes are particularly striking and combine well with chunky beads for a striking effect.

### EXPERT TIP

66 When forming coils, use flat-nose pliers with smooth jaws or nylon-coated pliers to prevent the wire from being dented. This is particularly important when you are using plated or coated wires. 99

# Question 183:
## How do I add texture to my coils?

Texture is added to coils by hammering. You will need a steel block to act as an anvil and a small hammer. Hammering is necessarily noisy and potentially damaging to your work surface. A folded towel or cork mat under the anvil will reduce noise and prevent damage. Tap coils gently with a rubber hammer to harden the wire and prevent them from bending out of shape. Use a metal chasing hammer to flatten areas or create dents on the surface.

If possible, hammer coils before adding beads, as you are likely to smash them otherwise. If you have to add the beads first — for example, if there are beads at the center of the coil or between halves of an s-shaped coil — then shield the beads as you hammer with a steel ruler or a wallpaper scraper.

When you are adding beads after hammering coils, make sure you do not hammer the wire where the bead will go, as it may become too wide to fit the hole of the bead. Try hammering coils in different ways on samples – use the edge of the hammer or the rounded end, or ensure the coil is entirely under the hammer for a totally smooth effect.

*BELOW* Use a ball-peen hammer to add a textured effect to your coils.

# Question 184:
# How do I make wire spirals?

Spirals are made by wrapping wire tightly around a mandrel to make a packed spring. A mandrel is essentially a rod; these can be bought in various cross-sections, or you can use a thick piece of wire or a knitting needle.

You can create spirals of assorted sizes by using various-sized knitting needles, or different-shaped spirals by using a variety of tools. Try a pencil to create a hexagonal spring, or buy a specialized mandrel in another shape – squares and triangles are readily available.

• Hold the tail of the wire in the palm of your hand with the end of the mandrel, and carefully twist the wire around the mandrel.

• Keep the wire tightly wound and tightly packed together.

• Keep the tension up in the coils, and then push them more closely together once you have finished.

• Slide the spring off the mandrel and trim the ends of the wire spring neatly to finish it. A spiral can be strung between beads to cover the stringing material, formed into beads, or simply hung from a wire loop as a charm.

*BELOW* Use a mandrel or tools of various shapes and sizes to create your spirals.

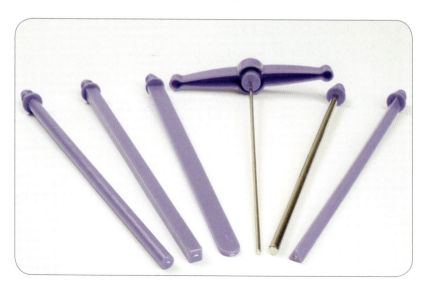

# Question 185:
# How do I create spiral beads?

To create a spiral bead, you will need to make a long thin spiral with fine wire. Create one at least 1.5–2 in. (4–5 cm) long with a very thin knitting needle or a mandrel.

- Slip the spiral off the mandrel, then trim the wire ends neatly.
- Leaving a tail for leverage, wrap a slightly thicker wire around the mandrel to create a spiral of four or five coils.
- Thread the original spring onto the wire above the coil and wrap it carefully around the mandrel to create a spiral with your spring.
- When you reach the end of the spring, wrap the core wire four or

five times around the mandrel to fix the bead, and then trim the loose ends.

- To create a spiral-wrapped bead, twist the ends of the spiral bead in opposite directions.
- Fit an oval bead inside the spiral, and thread the bead and spiral carefully onto an eye pin.
- Tighten the spiral around the bead and create a loop in the other end of the eye pin to complete the bead.

*BELOW* Spiral beads.

**186** How do I add beads to fabric?

**187** Can I make lines and curves with beads on fabric?

**188** How do I add decorative beading to evenweave fabric?

**189** Can I add beads to embroidery stitches?

**190** How do I attach sequins to fabric?

**191** Can I use sequins in jewelry?

**192** How do I get beads onto yarn?

**193** How do I knit with beads?

**194** Is it possible to add beads in crochet?

**195** How do I cover a large bead with seed beads?

**196** How do I create beaded tassels?

**197** What is French beading?

**198** Can I make beaded vessels?

**199** How do I make paper beads?

**200** How do I make polymer beads the same size and shape?

# 9

# OTHER WAYS TO USE BEADS

Beads are not limited to jewelry. In this chapter, we give you ideas for using your beads on fabric, making your own beads, and using sequins.

# Question 186:
# How do I add beads to fabric?

You can add beads to fabrics to enhance embroidery, create beautiful beaded fabric, or create beaded accessories. The easiest way to do this is to add beads with a single stitch, which allows you to dot them over fabric, disguise seams, outline motifs, or even completely fill a shape.

Use a short beading needle, which is easy to sew through fabric and is fine enough to go through seed beads. Always use a double thread to attach the beads, as this is far stronger, and attach thread securely with two tiny stitches on the back of the fabric rather than tying a knot.

## HOW IT'S DONE

**1** Take the thread through to the front of the fabric and pick up a bead.

**2** Lay the thread in the direction you want the bead to go, and take the bead back through the fabric. Make another stitch through the fabric and the bead.

**3** Move the needle to the next place you want a bead, and repeat the process.

**4** When you have finished you can make two tiny stitches again, or half-hitch around the previous thread twice to secure it or work a half-stitch.

# Question 187:
# Can I make lines and curves with beads on fabric?

You can use two basic embroidery stitches, couching or backstitch, to create lines or curves on fabric. The beads can be used to outline motifs, create flower stems, or make textured patterns. In couching, all the beads are strung on a thread before attaching; with backstitch, the beads are added a few at a time. Couching is ideal for straight or flowing lines and backstitch is better for tight curves.

*RIGHT* Couching is the technique for creating straight or flowing lines.
*FAR RIGHT* Backstitch is best used for tight curves.

## HOW IT'S DONE

### Couching

**1** Attach a thread securely to the back of the fabric with two small stitches, bring through to the front, and pick up enough beads to fill the line.

**2** Hold the thread taut, with the beads lying along the line, and secure the thread temporarily next to the last bead by wrapping it around a pin.

**3** Bring a second thread out between the second and third beads added.

**4** Take it over the laid thread between the beads and back into the fabric, creating a tiny invisible stitch. Add a tiny stitch after every few beads until you reach the end of the row.

**5** Take both threads through to the reverse side and secure the thread with two tiny stitches. On straight lines, you can space the stitches further.

### Backstitch

**1** Attach the thread securely to the back of the fabric, take the needle through to the front of the fabric, and then pick up five beads.

**2** Take the needle back through the fabric after the last bead, then bring it out between the third and fourth bead.

**3** Take the needle through the last two beads, then pick up the next five beads. Because the beads are held by more than one stitch, a smooth curve is created. For tight curves, use fewer beads to each stitch.

# Question 188:
# How do I add decorative beading to evenweave fabric?

Stitching on evenweave fabric (linen or aida) is usually worked diagonally, using either tent stitch, with a single diagonal in each "square" of fabric, or cross stitch, with two diagonals worked in each square. Beads added in tent stitch lie diagonally, whereas beads added with cross stitch lie with holes vertically. You can use a blunt needle as long as it will fit through the bead, and work the stitch over a block of aida or pairs of threads on linen. Beading on cross stich fabric is also called beadpoint.

### HOW IT'S DONE

**Tent stitch**

**1** Attach the thread to the back of the fabric with two small stitches, and take the needle through to the front of the fabric in the top corner of a block.

**2** Pick up a bead and pass through the diagonally opposite hole to complete the first stitch.

**3** Make a straight stitch at the back of the fabric to come back through directly to the left of the first hole.

**Cross stitch**

**1** Work a row of beaded tent stitches as above.

**2** After the last straight stitch across the base of the tent stitch, instead of forming the next tent stitch, take the needle back through the bead, adding a second diagonal stitch and completing the cross.

**3** Return along the row, crossing each stitch through the bead.

# Question 189:
# Can I add beads to embroidery stitches?

Ordinary embroidery stitches can be enhanced with beads – either the occasional bead dotted on the stitches, or fully beaded. Three stitches are outlined below.

Experiment with adding beads in different ways to create various effects, and use a variety of threads to match or contrast with your beads.

## HOW IT'S DONE

### Chain stitch

**1** Bring the needle through the fabric and pick up four beads.

**2** Pass back down through the fabric in the same place.

**3** Bring the needle back through the fabric inside the small loop you have created, pick up another four beads, and continue to create small loops – the end result will be a double row of seed beads.

**4** Fix the last stitch to the fabric with a tiny stitch over the thread between the second and third stitches.

### Fly stitch

**1** Bring the needle up through the fabric and pick up four beads.

**2** Create a loop by passing back through the fabric roughly two bead lengths from the original hole, then bring the needle back through the fabric inside the loop.

**3** Make a short straight stitch to make a y-shape with beads on the branches.

### Blanket (Buttonhole) stitch

**1** Bring the needle through the fabric and pick up two beads.

**2** Take the needle down the length of the stitch and across the width, then put it back through the fabric.

**3** Make a vertical stitch on the back of the fabric so that the needle comes out next to the two beads. The stitch should now be an l-shape.

**4** Pick up another two beads, and create another l-shaped stitch.

**5** Continue adding long and short l-shapes with beads, either on both parts of the stitch or on either part.

*TOP* Chain stitch worked with beads on every second stitch.

*MIDDLE* Fly stitch.

*BOTTOM* Blanket (buttonhole) stitch.

# Question 190:
# How do I attach sequins to fabric?

Sequins are often overlooked in beadwork, but they are bright, shiny, and attractive and can add a dramatic effect to your bead embroidery.

*RIGHT* Use sequins to add that extra special touch to your finished piece.

## HOW IT'S DONE

### Simple sequins

**1** If sequins are attached singly, you can use contrasting thread for a spoked effect or matching thread for an invisible effect.

**2** Bring the thread up through the center of the sequin, and then take it down over the rim and through the fabric.

**3** Repeat between two and five times, spacing the stitches evenly around the sequin.

### Beaded sequins

**1** Bring the needle up through the center of the sequin, and then pick up a small bead before returning through the center of the sequin. This effectively anchors the sequin to the fabric.

**2** For a more three-dimensional effect, pick up a bead before going through the sequin, then pick up a bead and return through both the sequin and the first bead.

### Row of sequins

**1** To attach a row of sequins, bring the needle up in the center of the first sequin, then make a stitch over the rim in the direction of the row.

**2** Position the next sequin so that it overlaps the first and covers the stitch, and then bring the needle out of the second sequin and so on.

**3** If the sequins form a loop, make sure the last sequin is added so that the stitch is hidden by the first.

# Question 191:
# Can I use sequins in jewelry?

There are two main ways to use sequins in beadwork – they can be added to fringe or used as beads to create chains. When being used in fringe or tassels, you can use the sequin as a turn bead, picking up seed beads and then the final sequin, then going back through the seed beads. This will give you a hanging disk on the end of the fringe, which will catch the light and give spectacular movement to earrings and bangles. An alternative, which will spread the fringes more and give a bulkier feel, is to add the sequin to a string of seed beads, then pick up another seed bead before going back through the sequin and the rest of the beads. This will hold the sequins horizontally, spacing the fringes widely at the ends. By placing the fringes closely together at the top, you will achieve a really flamboyant effect.

Alternatively, use pairs of sequins to sandwich a cheap, dull, wood bead to create a spectacular chain that can be wound around a wrist, or turned into a fabulous multistrand necklace.

*RIGHT* Sequins can be used as a hanging disk to catch the light and brighten up your earrings.

## HOW IT'S DONE

**1** Thread two needles and pick up a sequin, then a bead, then a sequin on one.

**2** With the other needle, go through the stack in the opposite direction, then pick up another sequin, bead, sequin stack.

**3** Take the other needle through in the opposite direction. The stacks should now lie next to one another.

**4** Add more stacks, taking the threads back and forth in a figure eight to create a long, stunning chain.

**Other Ways To Use Beads**

# Question 192:
## How do I get beads onto yarn?

Beads can be threaded directly onto yarn using a big-eye or twisted-wire needle (see Question 75). You can also tie a loop of thread to a beading needle and then pass the yarn through the loop of thread. The beads will then pass easily from the thread onto the yarn.

If the yarn is loosely spun, only thread a small quantity of beads at once, otherwise the yarn will fray as the beads are pushed down. Picking up single beads can be time consuming, but it allows you to create a pattern in the beads.

If you want to use a large number of beads, a bead spinner, which is a bowl on a spindle, can be used with a curved big-eye needle to pick up seed beads quickly onto thread or yarn. A bead spinner is like a small roulette wheel filled with beads; when spun, the motion forces the beads onto a special curved needle for easy threading. Use a mix of colors and sizes of seed beads if you want to create a random effect. If you want all the beads the same size and color, you can buy seed beads on strings, which can then be transferred onto yarn.

- Separate one string from the hank of beads and tie it with an overhand knot to the yarn.
- Carefully pass the first few beads over the knot and onto the yarn – the rest of the beads should easily follow over the flattened knot.

## EXPERT TIP

66 If you are using thick yarn and beads with small holes, you can string the beads onto cotton perle thread or crochet cotton thread and then knit the cotton perle alongside the thicker yarn, adding beads into the knitting as you go. Choose a thread that matches for an invisible way of adding beads, or a contrasting thread for a more eye-catching effect. 99

# Question 193:
# How do I knit with beads?

There are several techniques for knitting with beads but this method is the easiest. Add the beads on the back of the knitting, which is the right side. You can comfortably pre-string about 100–150 beads at a time, but if the yarn is very delicate, add fewer beads and join new threads each time you run out of beads.

- Cast on and knit two or three rows with no beads so that the wrong side of the work is facing, ready for adding the bead rows.
- Bring a few beads up into your hand, knit to where you want the first bead, and put the needle into the next stitch.
- Take one bead up to the back of the stitch and finish the stitch, securing the bead in the loop.
- Knit another few stitches and then add another bead. Continue to the end of the row and then knit the next row without beads.
- Add beads to every other row so that the beads are all on the right side of the fabric.

**Making a bag**
If you add beads on each row at the same stitch and then add progressively more beads to each stitch, you can increase the knitting – this is a lovely way to make beautiful little purses and bags.

- To increase the knitting, add single beads evenly spaced along the row, then on the next row add one bead between the same stitches to the end.
- On the next two rows, slide two beads up and knit the next stitch.
- Continue increasing the beads by one every two rows until there are about seven beads, then reduce the number of beads every two rows.
- Finish with a few rows of plain knitting to hold the work together.

To add beads on the front of the knitting, slip a stitch, then bring a bead up to the needle and knit the next stitch. The bead sits on the yarn that is carried in front of the slipped stitch.

# Question 194:
# Is it possible to add beads in crochet?

Adding beads to crochet is quite easy, as you simply bring a bead up to the work and then work the next stitch. Single crochet with craft wire is particularly successful with beads or even tiny semiprecious chips added on every stitch. You can create single or multiple strands to make quick and easy necklaces and bracelets. Crochet fabric in wire or yarn is also suitable for adding beadwork. With wire you generally keep to a basic single crochet, but with yarn you can try lots of different stitches. As the stitch height in crochet varies from stitch to stitch, the bead will sit in a different part of the crochet depending on the base stitch. Small washer-style beads work well with treble crochet, as the beads sit like little vertical bars. Adding a bead between every stitch creates an attractive heavy fabric.

You can also use a crochet hook to add occasional beads to knitting, which means that the beads don't need to be pre-strung.

*BELOW* Add beads to your crochet work.

# Question 195:
# How do I cover a large bead with seed beads?

You could use a large glass or wooden bead, but it may be very heavy by the time you have covered it in seed beads. Pressed cotton balls, which are available in a range of sizes, are a good alternative, as even large beads will still be relatively light.

## EXPERT TIP

**66 If you insert a knitting needle or similar rod through the pressed cotton ball, it will prevent the seed beads from going into the hole. 99**

## HOW IT'S DONE

**1** Paint the cotton ball using acrylic paint to match or contrast with your beads, and tie a thread through the hole in the ball. Pick up enough beads to reach from one end of the ball to the other, and then take the needle back through the center of the cotton ball.

**2** Keep adding rows of beads until you have gone all the way around the ball.

**3** Add shorter strands between the rows to fill in the gaps until the ball is completely covered.

**4** Secure the thread with a half-hitch knot before taking it through the ball and trimming the excess.

# Question 196:
## How do I create beaded tassels?

- Cut a piece of card to the length you would like your tassel to be, and wrap decorative thread around it until it reaches the required thickness.
- Cut along one edge and lay the threads out flat. Tie a thread tightly around the middle of the bundle.
- Fold the bundle in half and attach an eye pint to the thread loop.
- Pick up the tassel by the wire, and smooth the strands down over the tie and the bead.
- Cover a cotton ball with matching beads and thread the wire up through the center, holding the tassel tightly to the base of the beaded ball.
- Create a loop in the wire with round-nose pliers, and twist the free end of the wire around the stem to hold the tassel together securely.
- Cut off the excess wire, and attach the tassel to a cord or chain.

*BELOW* Add a touch of elegance with bead tassels.

# Question 197:
## What is French beading?

French beading is used to create three-dimensional structures, usually flowers, with seed beads and craft wire. You use a single length of wire with the seed beads threaded onto it. Don't cut the wire but work directly from the reel, stringing about 18 in. (45 cm) of seed beads before you begin.

*RIGHT* Keep adding rows of beads to make a perfect petal for your flower.

**HOW IT'S DONE**

**1** Make a tiny loop on the end of the wire to prevent the beads from slipping off, and then slide fifteen beads up to the tiny loop.

**2** On the other side of the beads, make a larger loop of wire around four fingers and carefully twist the loop to secure. The long strand of wire still attached to the reel is the working wire, and the 3 in. (8 cm) section with fifteen beads will be the center line of the petal.

**3** Bring a wire with sixteen beads alongside the center row, twist the wire around the top of the previous row, then bring the wire down the other side and slide up another sixteen beads.

**4** Keep adding rows of beads to the petal or leaf with one more bead until it is the right size.

**5** Make single loops and pieces of fringe to form the center of your flower and then arrange the petals together to form the actual structure, twisting all the wires together to make a stem.

# Question 198:
# Can I make beaded vessels?

Beaded vessels can be made using any beading technique that is firm enough to stand up unaided. You can use closely worked bead-weaving stitches such as herringbone, peyote stitch, or brick stitch, or incorporate wire into bead-loom weaving, knitting, or crocheting to create the structure. Here are three ideas:

## Bead weaving

You can make candle holder/cover/ luminary by working a circular base in herringbone stitch one bead larger than the base of your candle. When the base is the right size, stop increasing and continue herringbone to make straight sides that fit neatly over the tea light, covering the metal rim. You can use any seed beads for this with a strong beading thread.

## Wirework

Form a bowl shape with bent wires laid over a bowl like spokes. Weave colored wire in and out of the spokes, adding beads as you go along. When you have woven almost to the ends of the spokes, add beads to them and then coil the ends outward to create an attractive woven dish.

## Bead loom weaving

Use wire for the warps, adding two strands or a thicker wire on the outer edges so that the sides are stiff enough to support themselves. Make a cross shape and then fold up the sides to create a simple box.

*BELOW* Make a decorative candle holder for a unique gift.

# Question 199:
## How do I make paper beads?

Rolling tapered strips of paper has been used to make beads since Victorian times. Victorian ladies would cut wallpaper into long triangle shapes and roll them around knitting needles; the resulting beads would be strung on long threads and hung in doorways to create curtains.

*BELOW* Recycle your junk mail into attractive paper beads!

### HOW IT'S DONE

**1** To make beautiful paper beads for jewelry, cut tapered triangular shapes from magazines and catalogues (gardening catalogues are particularly good) or wrapping paper.

**2** Spread glue along the length, missing the first 0.5 in. (1.5 cm) at the thick end of the paper.

**3** Wrap the strip around a knitting needle, slide off carefully, and leave to dry.

**4** Add a layer of varnish to give shine to the bead.

**5** Make paper beads of different lengths and then use them to create fabulous jewelry!

# Question 200:
# How do I make polymer beads the same size and shape?

Slight irregularity in your beads may be attractive in some cases, making it clear that your beads are handmade; but if you want beads the same size, you can measure off exact quantities of clay. The easiest way to do this is to roll out clay in a long, tubelike shape, and then use a ruler as a guide to cut exact lengths of clay. These can be rolled and shaped to make a set of beads the same size. When you need a more professional look, or a set of perfectly graduated beads, you can use a bead roller.

Bead rollers are basically two sheets of plastic with corrugations of various sizes. You put the clay between the two layers and roll it back and forth to create a perfectly shaped bead. Because the roller has graduated sizes, you can make an entire matching set of beads for a necklace. It is also worth looking around for different shapes of bead roller, so that you can make your own professional quality tubes, bicones, and cones.

*BELOW* Polymer beads.

# Useful Information

## Glossary:

**2-drop** when two beads are used at the same time, but treated like one bead.

**Anneal** slowly cooling a glass bead in a kiln to give internal strength.

**Decrease** removing beads on a row to make your work narrower.

**Eye pin** a length of wire with loop at one end.

**Findings** metal pieces used to complete jewelry; earring wires, clasps, etc.

**Gauge (ga)** unit of measurement of wire thickness.

**Headpin** a length of wire with a wider end to prevent beads from falling off.

**Increase** adding beads to make your work wider.

**Mandrel** a rod (usually metal) used to form coils, or to support tubular bead stitches.

**Tension** how tight your work is.

## Web sites:

**U.S. (East Coast):**
www.tohoshoji-ny.com
www.afterglowbeads.com

**U.S. (West Coast):**
www.beadinspirations.com
www.beaditcolorado.com

**England:**
www.mailorderbeads.co.uk

**Scotland:**
www.beadshopscotland.co.uk

# Useful Information

## Bead Packaging

| Bead Width (mm) | Bead Size | Beads on 7.9-in. (20 cm) string | Beads in hank | Hank weight | Beads in 3-in. (8 cm) tube | Tube Weight |
|---|---|---|---|---|---|---|
| 3.3 | 6 | 200 | 2400 | 167 g | 150 | 13 g |
| 2.5 | 8 | 260 | 3120 | 100 g | 600 | 15 g |
| 2.2 | 9 | 300 | 3600 | | | |
| 2.0 | 10 | 320 | 3840 | | | |
| 1.8 | 11 | 340 | 4080 | 42 g | 1650 | 15 g |
| 1.3 | 15 | 480 | 5760 | 23 g | 3800 | 13 g |

## Wire Thickness

| mm | AWG | SWG | mm | AWG | SWG | mm | AWG | SWG |
|---|---|---|---|---|---|---|---|---|
| 4 | | 8 | 0.71 | | 22 | 0.212 | | 35 |
| 3.25 | | 10 | 0.7 | 21 | | 0.2 | 32 | 36 |
| 3 | | 11 | 0.63 | | 23 | 0.17 | | 37 |
| 2.65 | | 12 | 0.6 | 22 | | 0.15 | 34 | 38 |
| 2.36 | | 13 | 0.56 | | 24 | 0.132 | | 39 |
| 2 | 12 | 14 | 0.5 | 24 | 25 | 0.125 | | 40 |
| 1.8 | | 15 | 0.45 | | 26 | 0.112 | | 41 |
| 1.6 | | 16 | 0.4 | 26 | 27 | 0.1 | 38 | 42 |
| 1.5 | 14 | | 0.375 | | 28 | 0.09 | | 43 |
| 1.4 | | 17 | 0.315 | | 30 | 0.08 | | 44 |
| 1.25 | | 18 | 0.3 | 28 | | 0.071 | | 45 |
| 1.2 | 16 | | 0.28 | | 31 | 0.06 | | 46 |
| 1 | 18 | 19 | 0.265 | | 32 | 0.05 | | 47 |
| 0.9 | 19 | 20 | 0.25 | 30 | 33 | 0.04 | | 48 |
| 0.8 | 20 | 21 | 0.236 | | 34 | 0.025 | | 50 |

## Seed Bead Finish Abbreviations

| Abbr. | Bead type |
|-------|-----------|
| Tr | Transparent |
| Op | Opaque |
| T | Translucent<br>*(Greasy, opal or satin beads)* |
| L | Light color saturation |
| M | Medium color saturation |
| Dk | Dark color saturation |
| Dp | Deep color saturation |
| O/R | Opaque Rainbow |
| BL | Black-lined |
| Color/L | Color-lined |
| BrL | Brass-lined |
| CL | Copper-lined |
| SL | Silver-lined<br>*(Rocaille)* |
| SqH | Square hole |
| AL | Alabaster |
| AB | Aurora Borealis<br>*(Rainbow, Iris, Iridescent, and Fancy)* |
| Cy | Ceylon |
| M | Matte |
| Gloss | High shine |
| Lustre | Opaque with a pearly finish |
| M/R | Matte Rainbow |
| Met/R | Metallic Rainbow |
| Ghost | Matte rainbow metal lined |

## Bugle Sizes

| Bead Size | Czech Bugle Length | | Japanese Bugle Length | |
|-----------|------|--------|------|--------|
| | mm | inches | mm | inches |
| 1 | 2 | $^3/_{32}$ | 3 | $^1/_{10}$ |
| 2 | 4 | $^3/_{16}$ | 6 | $^1/_4$ |
| 3 | 7 | $^1/_4$ | 9 | $^3/_8$ |
| 4 | 9 | $^3/_8$ | | |
| 5 | 11 | $^7/_{16}$ | | |

## Birthstones

January: Garnet (red)
February: Amethyst (lilac)
March: Aquamarine (blue–green)
April: Diamond (white)
May: Emerald (green)
June: Pearl (cream)
July: Ruby (red)
August: Peridot (pale green)
September: Sapphire (blue)
October: Opal (iridescent)
November: Topaz (yellow)
December: Turquoise (turquoise)

## Necklace Lengths

Collar/choker: 12–16 inches (30–41 cm)
Princess: 17–19 inches (43–48 cm)
Matinee: 20–24 inches (51–61 cm)
Opera: 28–34 inches (71–86 cm)
Ropes: over 45 inches (138 cm)

# Index

## A
African helix 146
allergies 20, 32, 37, 62, 180
antique chains 67
antiquing 67

## B
backings 161, 162
bails 43
barrels 40
bead caps 52
bead diagrams 137
bead ends 121
bead-loom work, measuring 77
bead looming 150–173
bead looms 89, 152,
bead scoops 74
bead starts 121
bead stoppers 114
bead weaving 60, 75, 106–149, 154, 218
beaded vessels 218
beading boards 74, 77, 92
beading charts 116
beading cords 96
beading mats 74
beads 6–7, 10, 11
   natural 15
   quality 13
   shapes 12, 26
   storage 85
   weight 37
   wire wrapping 197, 198
bead-stringing wire, 65
birthstones 18, 223
bolt rings 38
bone beads 17
box clasps 41
bracelets 37, 41, 49, 64, 77
brick-stitch edging 168
bugle beads 24, 223
buttonholes 159

## C
calottes 47, 93
ceramic beads 19
chain 184, 185, 188
chain maille 45, 177, 186, 187
Charlotte beads 23
circular netting 140
circular pieces 119
clamshells 47
closed loop chains 183
coils 199, 200, 201
color saturation 28
cord ends 46, 61
crimp bars 157
crimp beads 50, 79
crimp covers 51
crimpimg 93, 94
crochet, adding beads 214
crystal beads 14, 94
cylinder beads 25

## D
daisy chain 147
directions 115

double-hook-and-eye findings 182
Dutch spiral 144

## E
Earrings 32, 33, 34, 35
   wires 36, 180
edging 168
elastic cord 63, 185
end bars 48, 49
end cones 46
extension chains 42
eye pins 44

## F
fabric 206, 208, 210
fabric cords 57
filigree patterns 190
findings 30–53
finishes 28, 28–29
fishhooks 180
fit, testing 77
freestyle bead weaving 137
French beading 217
French knitting 192
fringing 139, 140, 170 –173

## G
gemstones 18
gimp 51, 95
glass beads 13

## H
hammering 201
head pins 44
hex beads 24
horizontal netting 137, 138
horn beads 17

## I
illusion cord 60, 100
ivory 17

## J
jump rings 45, 69, 177, 179

## K
knitting 192, 213
knots
   figure-of-eight 103
   half-hitch 103, 110
   half-knot twist 104
   lark's head 103
   overhand 102
   reef 102
   sliding 101
   slipknot 103
   square 63
   square-flat 105
   surgeon's 103

## L
lampwork beads 13
large beads 11, 215
leather cord 56
lined beads 28–29
lobster clasps 38
loom work 130
   adding loops 169
   backing 161, 162
   bead weaving 154

beaded vessels 218
buttonholes 159
correcting 155, 164
creating patterns 156
edging 168
fastenings 159
fringing 170–173
shaping 160
thread ends 157
tubes 166
using wire 167
loop fastenings 158
loops 178, 181,182

## M
magnetic clasps 39
memory wire 64, 98
metal beads 20
metal-mesh tube 62, 97

## N
necklaces
   cord 96
   designing 92, 99–100
   findings 37
   floating 60, 100
   illusion 58
   memory wire 64
   multistrand 41, 46, 49, 99–100
   pearl 59
   standard lengths 42–43, 223
needles 86, 87, 88
   blunt 87, 163
   stuck 112
   threading 108
Nepal chain 148
nuts 16

## P
packaging 22, 222
painted beads 16
Pandora beads 13
paper beads 219
pearls 14–15, 59
pendants, hanging 181
picot edging 168
polymer clay beads 19, 220
pulled thread loom work 152, 163, 165

## R
regular loom work 152, 153, 157
rhino horn 17
ribbons 61, 97, 185
right-angle weave 133, 134, 135, 145
ropes 144

## S
St. Petersburg chain 149
screw clasps 40
seed beads 22, 23, 26, 27, 65, 215, 223
seeds 16
semiprecious stones 18
sequins 210, 211
S-hooks 40
skip beads 149
sliders 41
sliding knot fastenings 101
spacer bars 49

spiral beads 203
spiral cages 195
spiral rope 141, 142, 143
spirals 202
split rings 45
stamped filigree 53
stitches
   brick 117, 120, 121, 122, 145
   chain 136
   drop ladder 118
   embroidery 206–207, 208–209
   herringbone 117, 124, 125, 126, 145
   ladder 117, 118, 120, 122, 145
   multiple 117
   peyote 117, 127, 128, 129, 145
   shaping 121, 126, 129, 132
   square 117, 130, 131, 132
   starting 122, 123, 125
   twisted herringbone 126
   two-drop ladder 119, 124
stoppers 75
suede cord 56

## T
tassels 140, 216
tension 113, 114, 129
thread conditioners 58, 81, 114
thread zappers 81
threads 58, 59, 102, 108, 109
   adding 110
   finishing 110, 111, 157
   loose 78
toggle fastenings 158
toggles 40, 48
tortoise shell 17
tubes 144, 145
   African helix 146
   knitted 193
   loom work 166
tubular crimps 50
turn beads 149, 170

## V
vertical netting 139, 140
vintage beads 17, 21

## W
watches, beaded 48
wire 44, 65, 71
   bead stringing 94
   colored 69
   copper 68
   crochet 69, 194
   cutting 176
   knitting with 192
   loops 178
   silver 66, 68
   smoothing 80
   straitening 83
   thickness (gauge) 70, 222
   twisting 191
wire guardians 51
wire jigs 190
wire-wrapped fastenings 196
wooden beads 16

yarn, threading 212

zigzag spacers 189